The Organic Approach to Architecture

Deborah Gans and Zehra Kuz

 WILEY-ACADEMY

Acknowledgements

This book began as a symposium, funded by Pratt Institute School of Architecture with the generous support of its dean, Thomas Hanrahan. We thank Kenneth Frampton for his initial insights and commentaries that contributed much to the symposium's orchestration. The series of events at various locations was made possible through Pratt Institute's technical resources and assistance. Erdal Akdag designed the symposium graphics. An exhibition accompanied the symposium whose production was only possible by Matthew Jelacic's effort. We were very grateful to receive a Graham Foundation Grant, which ultimately enabled us to document the experience.

The book would not have been possible without the continued contribution of the symposium participants who supplied valuable documentation of their work and research. The design concept of Rita Bertolini has given the book a graphic presence in great sympathy with its content. For the photographic documentation of Hans Scharoun's work, the time and talent of Mete Demiriz is greatly appreciated. Finally, we have had the pleasure of working with an enthusiastic team of editors from Wiley-Academy, beginning with our discussions about publication with Maggie Toy and continued in our collaboration with the editors Abigail Grater and Mariangela Palazzi-Williams. We hope that the book is as provocative for our readers as it was for us in the making. *Deborah Gans and Zehra Kuz*

Photo credits: Every effort has been made to locate sources and credit material, but in any cases where this has not been possible, our apologies are extended. Unless otherwise stated, all illustrations are courtesy of the architects.

Cover: Haresh Lalvani, *Morphogenetic Pathway*

Other Wiley Editorial Offices

Contents

Deborah Gans

Introduction:
Goethe's Fish

The conference that forms the basis of this book originated with Zehra Kuz and my desire to address certain current problematic conditions of architecture in relation to its environments: the natural environment, the megalopolis and its concomitant sprawl, and the virtual environment in relation to these physical contexts. We gathered together a range of practitioners, historians and theorists from various fields who could redress reductive interpretations of context, *Zeitgeist* scenarios produced through these readings and the formalisms claimed to address them. With a sense of duty to a tradition that exceeded our sense of trepidation, we named our endeavour and its largest context of thought, the organic. Our initial hesitation came from the abuse of the word which the conference set out to examine. After quite some time reflecting on how the issues touched upon during the course of the conference might be brought together to suggest an armature on which to hang the organic, the following series of categories emerged as both a chronology and a set of ideas.

The Dynamic of Form

The value of the organic pervades all western architectural theory, not in a specific figural body but in a natural philosophy associated with Giordano Bruno, which conceived of the universe as an organism and the work of architecture as an organic operation. This attitude underlies Alberti's description of structure as sinews and ligaments working together and Palladio's concept of

Fish

Photo credit:
Francesca Pfister

the villa plan as a digestive system of service spaces functioning in support of the placid physiognomy of the served. However, it is in the work of both English and Germanic thinkers at the turn of the 19th century, namely William Taylor Coleridge and Goethe, that the contemporary sense of organicism, and the term organic, first appear as dynamic rather than static concepts of nature in both artistic and scientific terms. Goethe's project, the understanding of form as being inclusive of the natural and the man-made, the scientific and poetic, makes him a touchstone for outlining this new proposition.

For Goethe, the botanist, the total form or gestalt of an organism accounts for the complexity of its life cycle as it gradually develops, yet somehow retains its identity.[1] Coleridge underlines that it is 'the innate, the development from within that distinguishes the organic from the mechanic operation'.[2] According to this genetic model, any static composition understood as a single moment wrested from temporality is impoverished even more than it is incomplete. As Goethe writes of Cologne Cathedral in his memoirs, 'for an unfinished work is like one destroyed'.[3] Form is forming, as projected through the semantics of the German, *buildung*, yet the trajectory of the forming must be complete. Goethe continues, 'I sadly sank myself into this frozen world edifice, arrested in the midst of creation and far from completion. Here was an immense thought that had not come into execution, as if architecture were there to persuade us that by many men, in a series of years nothing can be accomplished . . .'[4] This tension between the forming and the form, its becoming and being, or its process and unity, is a new use of dialectic. Classical dialectic was in itself dynamic, a method of scrutiny that used analogics, oppositions, and transformations in its attempt to harness the ever-shifting physical world in the search for truth; but the truth classical dialectic sought was static, an unchanging world of ideas. In Goethe's monism, the dialectical movements between inner and outer form, spirit and matter are themselves truths lodged within nature and artistic production.

The Environmental Factor

According to Goethe's science, 'as inner form is not separable from outer form, neither is organism from environment.'[5] Rather, a constant interchange takes place so that the single organism is in some sense a 'pluralism' of conjoined elements continuous with its surroundings. Identity means the persistence of patterns within the flux of time and boundary. Goethe calls this stability of relations 'ur' type, as in archetype or prototype, not to be confused with the Cartesian sense of structure or truth as lying behind experience.[6]

Function

The habitual distinction between form and function has no reality in Goethe's description of experience. Function is 'existence thought of as an activity', a patterning of behaviours through which they attain 'good form'.[7] In this often cited passage from *Italian Journey*, Goethe posits the origin of architecture as the spatial imprinting of behaviour in a way that persists as form while allowing for further and more developed interaction:

> When something worth seeing is taking place on level ground everybody crowds forward to look: those in the rear find various ways of raising themselves to see over the heads of those in front; some stand on benches, some roll up barrels; some bring carts on which they lay planks cross-wise; some occupy a neighbouring hill. In this way in no time they form a crater. Should the spectacle be oft repeated in the same spot, makeshift stands are put up for those who pay, the rest manage as best they can. To satisfy this universal need is the architects' task. By his art he creates as plain a crater as possible and the public itself supplies the decoration. Crowded together its members are astonished in themselves. They are accustomed at other times to seeing each other running hither and thither in confusion, bustling about without order or discipline. Now this many headed, many minded fickle, blundering monster sees itself united in one noble assembly, welded into one mass, a single body animated by a single spirit.[8]

Deborah Gans

The Empathic Subject/Object Relation

In describing this continuity of object, environment and behaviour, Goethe does not commit what Coleridge calls the 'sophism of mistaking the conditions for causes'.[9] According to Goethe, 'the fish isn't fashioned for water nor does it adapt itself to water; rather, the fish exists in and through water'.[10] This reciprocity of organism and environment defines also the relations of subject to object, including the act of perception.

Beginning with his own science, in essays such as 'Experiment as a Mediator between Subject and Object', Goethe observes how he as the subject observer affects the object observed. This mutual effect can unite things in the instant as an *aperçu*, or in the act of intuitive contemplation as an *anschauung* that combines reasoning about a thing with responsiveness to it. At the boundary of his own subjectivity, Goethe finds that, 'Everything forces itself upon me, I no longer ponder upon it, it comes out to meet me'[11] and forges there a unity of nature based on experience.

Struggle for Existence

Goethe's unity of nature is then a matter of relationships, which produce death and destruction as often as life and creation.[12] The principles governing the connections among all organisms and phenomena are polarisation (whether it repels or attracts) and subordination. Coexistence without horizontal polarity and vertical subordination is merely the absence of relation and therefore the absence of order or form, without which there is also no possibility for meaning.

Morphology

It was Goethe who coined the term and discipline of morphology, the study of form, which, although he began by examining the transformations of plants, he understood as a general science. His search for form in the face of Romanticism's formlessness led him from botany to principles that he believes describe all forming, to the degree that certain distinctions between the organic and inorganic become moot. His art, science and poetry are a search for form out of the flux in all aspects of existence. What distinguishes art and architecture from other forming is its intentionality, or *gehalt* (in addition to its *gestalt*), which creates significance or meaning.

Evolution as Transformation

Taken together, these strains of Goethe's thinking presage the physical organic theory that came to dominate our time – Darwinism – a debt acknowledged by

Darwin himself in *Origin of the Species*.[13] In *Origin*, genetically inherited characteristics, which we may liken to Goethe's persistence of form, are shaped by the struggle for survival, a variant on Goethe's dynamic antagonism, so that those individuals most empathic or environmentally responsive come to be naturally selected. Darwin proposes a forceful individuality, independent of even Goethe's 'ur' type, when he asserts there are no species but rather moments of shape and stability within an ongoing transformation that can occur through the smallest of particular variations. These variations are, in themselves, random; and their persistence within form is contingent on their immediate environment. In Darwin's description of the environmental factor, the empathic, expansive impulse of Goethe encounters the self-limiting one of Malthus, who posits as nature's rule the condition that more individuals are produced than the environment can support.[14] As Darwin sees it, the ensuing struggle for available resources is not simply brutal. He writes, 'I should premise that I use struggle for existence in a metaphorical sense including dependency of one being on another and including (which is more important) not only the life of the individual but success of leaving progeny.'[15] The struggle to survive as the simultaneous engagement of all individuals connects nature in a unity that is in its totality and process beautiful. Darwin explains:

> The structure of every organic being is related in the most essential yet often hidden manner to that of all other organic beings with which it comes into competition . . . It is a truly wonderful fact – the wonder of which we are apt to overlook from familiarity – that all animals and plants throughout all time and space should be related to each other in group subordinate to group, in the manner which we everywhere behold . . . From so simple a beginning endless forms most beautiful and most wonderful have been and are being evolved.[16]

Historical Constraint and Romantic Freedom

As Darwin projects a scientific and natural version of Goethe's dynamic form, so Hegel projects a cultural one. In Hegel's narrative, art is made for man's sensuous apprehension in such a way as to address itself ultimately to his mind.[17] The mind dragged through matter produces a dialectical struggle, between the sensual and the idea, that is the form and content of art. As with Goethe's fish, art does not imitate nature, and nature is not the cause or content of art; rather, art is the struggle to re-present the self through nature and in relationship to it – an organic operation. According to Hegel, the Gothic cathedral looks like a forest only incidentally, as a secondary effect of the degree to which human beings animate the stone by producing ornament, which then resonates empathically with the life spirit itself.

Because art struggles to reconcile foundational opposites of sensation and mind, its truth is unstable. The larger teleological movement towards pure mind

Deborah Gans

periodically upsets the relationship of sense and spirit, or form and content, that we know as style, and art moves on – again and again. As in Darwinian evolution, the legacy of all that has gone before appears not as ideals to be copied but as a series of historical constraints that have shaped the present. To summarise the dialectical movement of historical constraint as Hegel sees it: 'Symbolic art seeks the perfect unity of form and content that classic art finds and romantic art transcends.'[18] Rather than formlessness, this romantic art displays the power of the subjective spirit to dissolve what it penetrates. Expressed in the Gothic cathedral rising in a pinnacle to a concentration at a single point, from which emerges the peal of bells in a vibration of no dimension, the goal of art is freedom, the transparent form of feeling.

Technological Relativism and Determinism

Based on a Hegelian belief in the relativistic value of historical form, the search for an architecture of its time came to dominate mid-19th century Europe. Despairing of architecture's relationship to both nature and the city in the face of the degradations of the Industrial Revolution, Viollet-le-Duc, Victor Hugo and John Ruskin, among others, posit tools as the Hegelian extension of mind on to matter, and technology as the force of cultural change. They seek models of total organisation and *Zeitgeist*, or the unified expressivity of material culture. They identify particular historical moments, most notably the Gothic, when the dynamic tension between man and his tools generated this kind of working synthesis of society and the means of production, of mind and matter, and of individual and community. As Ruskin wrote in *The Nature of the Gothic*, contrasting the organicism of the medieval guild to the mechanism of industrial labour, 'you must either make a tool of the creature or a man of him'.[19]

Art and Experience

Adopting Darwin's assertion that randomness of production and contingency of history underlie change, John Dewey breaks free of Hegel's transcendental purpose. Using Hegel's sense of culture as embodied thinking, Dewey addresses the issue of intention or meaning which is disregarded in Darwin's mechanical continuity of man and beast. From this 'marriage of Hegel and Darwin'[20] he forges a description of *experience* as the totality and the dynamic of man's relation to nature. According to Oliver Wendell Holmes, who along with William James is Dewey's precursor in pragmatic thinking, 'Experience is that which arises out of the interaction of the human organism with its environment: beliefs, values, intuitions, customs prejudices – the "felt necessities of the time".'[21]

For Dewey, good experience is art. Good experience occurs where means and end, process and product, the 'instrumental' and the 'consummatory' are related. Bad experience, on the other hand, is characterised by the displacement of means from ends (as in work valued for its wage), which then separates meaning from both activity and receptivity. Dewey's illustration of this principle in the building of a house as art is fortuitous here:

> To a person building a house, the end-in-view is not just a remote and final goal to be hit upon after a sufficiently great number of coerced movements have been duly performed. The end-in-view is a plan, which is contemporaneously operative in selecting and arranging materials. The latter, brick, stone, and mortar are means only as the end-in-view is incarnate in them, in forming them. The end-in-view is present at each stage of the process; it is present in the meaning of the materials used and acts done; without its informing presence, the latter are in no sense means they are extrinsic causal conditions. The statement is generic; it applies at every stage. The house when complete is 'end' in no exclusive sense. It marks the conclusion of certain organization of certain materials and events into effective means; but these materials and events still exist in causal interaction with other things. New consequences are foreseen; new purposes, ends-in-view, are entertained; they are embodied in the coordination of the thing built, now reduced to material, along with the other materials, and thus transmuted into means . . .[22]

Rehearsing the argument of Goethe's fish (the persistence of internal structure within the flux of environmental exchange) Dewey's house at the moment of its effective birth from material has a form which, subsequently, over the life of the house, returns to material that is formed again. The house fluctuates between means and end, condition and cause.

Futurism

According to the principle of art as experience, historical relativism is more accurately a kind of Futurism in which supplanted cultural moments become inaccessible or mere 'absence'. Science is the practice of knowledge found within experience. The past has an identity separate from ourselves that we nevertheless reach into and, by so doing, tamper with in a search for meaning that science does not provide. Dewey exhorts us 'to turn our faces to the future',[23] not because that is where utopia resides exactly but because truths and values emerge in the process of getting there.

The Context of Democracy

'The work of art is the truly individual thing'[24] but, from the point of view of Goethe's fish for whom nothing exists in isolation, it takes its form only through interaction with its conditions. The largest context of human experience – the

Deborah Gans

social – is likewise the necessary field of development for the individual. The autonomous individual is mere abstraction. Dewey describes how the self comes into being through its assertion in the community – as action. The forming of the individual is achieved as she observes, experiments and tests her truth with others as part of a 'community of inquiry'. Democracy is both the process of, and the environment for, shaping provisional truths. Goethe's Hellenized theatre is a physical trace of such a democratic forming, in which the situation of the actor before an audience creates a mirror for self and community, and a condition of social connectivity. This space in turn is a generator for future enactment, a 'space of appearance' so named by Hannah Arendt, 'where individuals encounter each other as equals'.[25]

Pluralism

In a critique of the collectivity of fascism and communism, Dewey asserts that participatory democracy does not require homogeneity or standardisation, mass culture or conformity, but allows for a pluralism that can acknowledge different root cultures as well as individual preferences. In the Jeffersonian manner, it requires only that the individual, educated in methods of scientific inquiry, participates in the creation of a local public and in doing so identifies herself. Attempting to redress the disintegration of American individualism based on a now-defunct frontiersmanship, and fearing the subsequent Americanisation of the world, Dewey argues that industrialised society, if released from its false monolithic, institutional bondage, can offer new forms of organisation by multiple associations, namely a 'pluralism of laws, industries, politics, arts, educations and philosophies'.[26] Organisation (even corporate organisation) 'as in any living organism, is the cooperative consensus of multitudes of living cells, each living in exchange with others'.[27]

Plasticity, Folds and Antiformalism

This 'organic unity of experience', as Dewey unapologetically describes it, models the ways in which we transform truths over time. According to William James, 'New truth is always a go-between, a smoother-over of transition. It marries old opinion to new fact to show a minimum of jolt, a maximum of continuity . . . To a certain degree, therefore, everything here is plastic.'[28] The plastic state is a way station within the extreme fluidity of truth, where facts 'interpenetrate', as Hilary Putnam describes it, with the theory and value of the facts.

Plasticity plays out as an interpenetration of material and technology, object and its model of production, means and end, in the writings of Frank Lloyd Wright who attributes the term to his teacher, Louis Sullivan. Wright explains plasticity as 'physical continuity, used as a practical working principle within the very nature of the building itself'.[29] Its constructive principles are material continuity in lieu of joinery, and structural continuity in lieu of a separation of parts according to a separation of forces. Rather than resolve the application of force to material in a mechanical hinge or a material joint, the plastic form absorbs the impact within its surface, either through the use of a 'monomaterial' such as reinforced concrete, or through the spatial vision of the 'folded plane' changing in direction without a break.

Plasticity is also the compression of form and function into a simultaneous action, described by Wright in the literally organic condition of 'expressive flesh covering the skeleton as contrasted with the articulation of the skeleton itself'.[30] Plastic solutions overcome the discontinuity between the functional element of the structure and the form of its cladding, and thereby the discontinuity between the environments of inside and outside, man and nature, individual and community. The vehicles for this overcoming include the concrete cantilever but also the glass wall – 'like crystallised air'.

Plasticity is antiformalism in that it resists autonomy, discontinuity and systems in themselves – hence it resists language. It is endemic to the more Darwinian aspects of organicism, including Goethe's morphology and pragmatism, to see language as a substratum of nature and experience with which it is continuous, rather than to see form as a substratum of language connected to nature only through intentionality. In lieu of an autonomous grammar, Wright offers the 'shape-relation between the various elements that enter into the constitution of the thing',[31] whatever they may be. According to this organic approach, transformation within architecture and art occurs without commitment to a specific language or to the ideology of invention. 'The object is an object of manipulation rather than the embodiment of either telos or logos, such that its truth is its expediency.'[32]

There are grounds that contemporary formalisms and organicism share, namely a sceptical relation to foundational truth and to rationalism, that leads both of them to a dependence on process. But formalism depends on an internalised logic followed from its original premise – a tendency to Cartesian method – while the pragmatist sees process as the expedient means directed, at any moment, to an ends-in-view – in other words, as practice.

Linguistic Retooling

Current neopragmatists find Dewey's concept of experience unable to cope with the weakness of our democratic context because it does not sufficiently account for the relationship between subject and object, language and the world. Richard Rorty, a prime enunciator of neopragmatic subjectivity, suggests that we might employ different languages in expedient ways as tools of different explorations: namely the Derridian languages of metaphor for the private self, and banal speech for the negotiation of the public realm. He sees the potential for a new kind of pluralism in 'the contrast between the private need for autonomy and the public need for a synoptic view of the goals of a democratic society'.[33] For

Deborah Gans

others, this dichotomy treads close to the old split of mind (private) and matter (public) and to a formalism in which languages with internalised behaviour function almost mechanistically, as 'algorithms' or 'programs' as Rorty calls them, within bounded realms of public and secret. As an alternative, Hilary Putnam posits the ordinary as the place where many language games occur in such a way that the boundary of the individual and the community is fluid and shifting. Claiming late Wittgenstein as an ally in his description of the plasticity of language he quotes: 'In time the banks and the river may change places.'[34] Putnam likewise connects language games to our different practices like science, religion and architecture or 'forms of life', as Wittgenstein called them, in such a way that even when we stand outside another's game we bridge the gap through empathy. In this understanding of humanness as lodged in all human behaviour, some of which exceeds the limits of language, he reasserts the interwoven action of mind and body and environment, and invokes Goethe's assertion that 'in the beginning was the act'[35] (not the word).

Architecture, which in its organic capacity traditionally sought the binding of individual to collective, of nature to culture, and of prelinguistic to linguistic form even as it conceived itself to be the agent of change from the former states to the latter, has for decades now played out the dissociation of these pairings. The architect asks, 'What is the public space of Rorty's democratic utopia where the political is a matter of short-term compromise aimed at "simply being left alone?"' and stakes out alternative positions such as Eisenman's exercise of Derridean formal logic to shape a collective dream of space, or Koolhaas's displacement of the public subject of urbanism to within typology, where the 'anything goes' autonomy of the self can happen within the banality of the 'generic' big box 'whose subtext is *fuck* context'.[36] The volatile realisation of Dewey's fears – 'bigness'[37] and the late-capitalist Americanisation of the globe – in combination with Rorty's truth – expanding autonomy – have rendered the interweaving of mind, body politic and environment so inexpedient that, despite our parlance of connectivity, Günter Behnisch has concluded that, 'our time is not organic. There is no organic architecture for our time'.

Connectivity: Loom, Knot, Net

Connectivity is the now-pervasive term used to describe our desired states of mental and mechanical functioning, and spatial and natural contexts; it is also the persistent diagram for organic form. Even Goethe derives his diagram for the organic not from plant form but from the connective structure of the loom. The warp and weft are the armature for the individual continuities of the threads whose interweaving opens up the dialectical foundation of the loom into a multiplicity of relationships. Following on Goethe, the 19th-century architect and theorist Gottfried Semper describes architecture as the textile dressing of a skeletal frame upon a hearth as found in the 'ur' condition of the Bedouin tent and then, reiteratively, in the dressing of masonry, and – we might project – in the curtain wall. In Semper, the rectilinear armature of the loom imaginatively translates into the structural framework from which the textile wall is hung. This separation of the textile from its loom frees it from Goethe's armature of warp and weft, and suggests alternative weavings some of which rely exclusively on other threads for connectivity – as in a knot or net. Semper illustrates this knot which he calls 'the oldest technological sign' first as a thread turned in upon itself, and then in relation to another.[38] Although incomplete as enclosure or architecture, the knotted textile is simultaneously a surface and a structure, hence plastic in the Wrightian sense that it responds to applied force through material deformation rather than through a break across a discrete joint. Its multiplicity of knots is a productive redundancy, ensuring that failure of the part is not the unravelling of the whole.

Current diagrams of 'net' critique this organic model from within. In its Deleuzian mode the tent becomes felt, which is pressed from unstructured fibres rather than woven. Detached from its 'ur' hearth within the 'repelling' landscape of the desert, this architecture becomes a smooth surface with no apparent armature.[39] Networks of communication are likewise smooth surfaces in that they dissolve the delineation of private/public and the very boundary of the individual in a seamless interface of subject and information, contiguity and feedback.[40] Deployed by architects such as Asymptote, the surface of information takes on a reach that is simultaneously 'ecological and narcissistic' to use Baudrillard's terms, where everything must stay in contact and be informed of the respective condition and position of everything else in the system. The extension of such a network in a totalising connectivity over all information and environments, both artificial and natural, has the paradoxical effect of obliterating their distinctions. The current rendering of architecture by Bos and van Berkel as a landscape of undulating surfaces plays out the absorption of nature into the ever-expanding network of late capitalism in that it self-admittedly operates as a formal means of seduction, an artifice whose utility is to fabricate 'effect, desire and demand'.[41] The reversed position, in which the network of nature absorbs artifice, is the position of extreme ecology, where the decentred human being has no more power or purpose than fish in the functioning of the whole. Greg Lynn's cyberanimism mimics this functional economy of man-made and natural operations in its mutations of biomorphic shapes pulled by Goethian fictive magnetic forces; but molecular-level technologies, as they appear with sci-fi realism in John Johansen's nanotech growing house, are the real site of collapse of organic and inorganic processes.

Other versions of network resist the endgame scenario of collapse into the single mother-net by stressing behaviour as form and our ability to shape that behaviour. They identify superconnectivity or overnetworking as a source of an overinternalisation that is detrimental to the net's adaptive, resilient and evolutionary behaviours. This neopragmatic net encourages weak links as well as strong ones, failures, noninstrumentalised or autonomous nodes, small aristocratic clusters as well as democratically dispersed singularities and conflict, in a neo-Darwinian sense.[42] It bases its legitimacy as an organic paradigm on its

Deborah Gans

role as science's most prevalent tool for description, whether yeast protein inter-
actions or river flows. As applied by eco-idealists in their small-world planning, and architects like Richard Rogers in his compact city of multivalent
contact, the neopragmatic net offers a model for a complexly wired public
realm.[43] It critiques both the mass-mind of the 'swarm' and the self-limiting
agreements of Rorty's 'synoptic concord' as being immune to the importance of
conflict.[44] From the point of view of this net's proponents, without the ability
to admit direct forms of struggle into the public realm or a holistic vision we
face the threat of environmental and social disaster.

In all the scenarios just presented, the organic approach begins with the
acknowledgement of just how 'unfashionable' the situation of architecture is –
like that of Goethe's fish (who is unfashioned for water but exists through and
in it). It requires the architect-as-form-giver to ask how the architectural object,
as a matter of form, engages 'in' its material and 'through' its social production and how it then persists.

The Event

The presentations in the first symposium, 'Evolution and Lines of Descent',
described an organic descended from German Idealism and Romanticism, by
way of Zehra Kuz's interpretation of the historical figures of Hugo Häring,
Hans Scharoun and Jean Gebser to the living presences of Günter Behnisch and
Volker Giencke. This lineage was then balanced in the second symposium,
'Transformations', by the culture of American panellists such as William
Katavolos and John Johansen, both of whom are steeped in the liberal democratic thinking that underlies Frank Lloyd Wright's organic and its subsequent
technological variants from Buckminister Fuller onwards to Haresh Lalvani.

In fact, throughout the conference, cross-continental play filled the conver-
sations, as Behnisch invoked Horatio Greenough and Wright, Katavolos quoted
Riegl and bashed Dewey, Johansen quoted Hegel, Kuz invoked George Simmel,
Brigham used Wittgenstein, Dalland turned to Frei Otto, Giencke spoke of his
elective affinity with Archigram and Frank Gehry, and Frampton presented a
hybrid history of architectural production. Together they suggested an alternative lineage of the modern, not just through the status of alternative figures
such as Johannes Duiker or Lois Welzenbacher but through their questioning
of our received understandings of terms such as function and gestalt. Whatever
the flaws in its compressed narrative, the first part of this introduction traced
a lineage for the organic concocted by the totality of the panels, and categorised
the hooks of thought presented by the panellists whose contributions are set
out briefly below.

The keynote address of Günter Behnisch offered a vision of 'art as experience' where the connection of 'means and ends' practised in his office
established the value of the architectural product. His community of design
became a kind of existential and utopian proposition for the conference against

which the other contexts were measured: whether Zehra Kuz's society of free encounter, Ahmet Omurtag's community of random event and Brighams' familial forms of life, all of which argued for the sustenance of organic society, or Giencke's mourning for the loss of Scharoun's Berlin, Frampton's elegy for the Wrightian landscape of participatory democracy and Katavolos's simultaneously seductive and unnerving vision of extreme individuation, which all argued against.

While there was some suggestion by Behnisch that, in the literal transparency of glass and the phenomenal transparency of fragmentation, architecture can become a linguistic and instrumental '*frei arkitektur*' of democracy, he and Kenneth Frampton also problematised the relation of form and function, autonomy and social utility. Zehra Kuz reconsidered form as forming, using the precedents of Häring and Scharoun to set out the formative role of environmental and behavioural factors and the formative power of experience as organised by the viewer. She expanded the idea of the empathic to a contemporary theory of perception, using Gebser's a-perspectival space as a social reading of contemporary geometries and experience. Following Kuz's play with architecture's mediation of subject and object, Eeva Pelkonen took up the camera as a tool of organic perception and construction of space in the hands of Alvar Aalto. This fundamental tension of form and forming was then framed in biological terms by Ahmet Omurtag, who described the organism's struggle to survive in an 'unenchanted' landscape or environment 'unfashioned' to it.

Omurtag's philosophy of organic behaviour underscored the Darwinian and Goethian themes of identity and change in relation to environmental factors taken up in the next symposium, on transformation. Haresh Lalvani presented a genetic code of form that contained all past, present and possible geometries. He described a connectivity that, while completely internal to the system, allows for translation to material production through its digital encoding, and thus for the interpenetration of virtual and material contexts. Tom Brigham first showed morphing (as distinguished from Lalvani's morphology) to be a dynamic of form in which change is totally internal and shift in identity is complete, but he then described how this seemingly autonomous transformation engaged other contexts of meaning. He described transforming families of silverware as a Wittgensteinian 'form of life', that is to say as a game of perception and the physical body, the goal of which is to create culturally conditioned 'cognitive modules'. As Lalvani's morphology connects to material, so Brigham's connects to social practice.

The transformation of the architectural object in terms of its forming or organisation, its operation and its environmental responsiveness, was also discussed. Mahadev Raman and Todd Dalland both demonstrated how digital modelling creates an environment and behaves organically by simulating the dynamic relation between internal constraints, such as strength of material or humidity control, and external ones, such as wind or climate. While Raman argued that no one formal language fulfils the desired relation of factors, Todd Dalland made a pitch for the lightness and movement found in his own tents

Deborah Gans

as ecological and hence moral qualities, required by our increasingly fragmented and ephemeral city. His buildings are literally 'transformers', which pack up and move through a continuous landscape of 'tree stump' infrastructure hook-ups. Volker Giencke likewise spoke of our desire for mobility and the nomadic condition as they are implicit within his more traditionally sited architecture. Seeing his own work as the extension of the freedoms in Scharoun's loose urban landscape, he spoke of the transparency of his botanical greenhouses not as the disappearance of form but as the dissolution of functional boundaries. His talk was a paean to the way glass skins transform as they respond to atmospheric states of light and to climate. Providing the most strictly biological interpretation of responsiveness, John Johansen described the building as a body, organised as systems and organs that perform responsively to internal and external pressures in order to maintain dynamic stability. Extending the vision of a digitally programmable building to its logical conclusion, he and William Katavolos have long envisioned an artificial organic or chemical architecture based on the material encoding of nanotechnologies. For Katavolos, this chemical architecture is but one aspect of our larger drive towards superindividuation, seen also in the phenomenon of customised mass production. It ends with the man who becomes his car, a vision of superindividuated customised production that reciprocally instrumentalises both the world and the body.

This talk of transformation as the dissolution of formal boundaries, as mobility and environmental responsiveness begged the question of the larger contexts in which these behaviours occur, as was taken up in the last symposium, 'Organ-i-city'. John Johansen described individual buildings as temporary by-products within the city tissue of individual and collective action. While supportive of Johansen's vision of the active body-collective, Frampton argued against the collapse of the artificial and organic, which he saw as the endgame of commodification, and for a dialectical understanding of nature and culture that is synthesised rather than overcome through architectural production. His history of the organic was also a warning against the organic tendency to privilege nature over urbanism, science over history, anarchic individualism over culture and the vernacular over the self-conscious. Despite these reservations, he offered 'organic environmental culture' as his critique of current sprawl as a kind of pathological growth. It took the form of an homage to Aalto's fusion of landscape and urban density, while still questioning the ability of the current built form/landform blurs to achieve the collective structures and physical monumentality fundamental to a true urbanism. The discussion ended as it began in Ahmet Omurtag's framing of nature from the organism's point of view when he stated: 'The world is a fatal environment, not because it is malicious but because inanimate nature is indifferent and does not 'care about' the complex arrangements that organisms need in order to live. One could say that organisms live in a disenchanted environment.' While playing with the dream of an enchanted landscape, the conference searched for the insight needed to avoid the proliferation of indifference.

Notes

1. Elizabeth Wilkinson, 'Goethe's Conception of Form' in Victor Lange (ed), *Goethe; a collection of critical essays*, Prentice-Hall (Englewood Cliffs), 1984, p 121. In Goethe's words: 'For the whole complexity of existence of an actual being, German has the word Gestalt.'

2. William Taylor Coleridge, lecture note in Harold Bloom and Lionel Trilling (eds), *The Oxford Anthology of English Literature*, Oxford University Press, 1973, p 656.

3. Johann Wolfgang von Goethe, trans RO Moon, *Poetry and Truth from My Life*, Alston Rivers (London), 1912, p 552.

4. Ibid.

5. Wilkinson, op cit, p 121. In this passage, Wilkinson writes a beautiful summary of Goethe's environmental principles and his vocabulary, which we so identify with the organic today.

6. For an extended discussion on Goethe's idea of type see Willy Hartner, 'Goethe and the Natural Sciences' in Victor Lange (ed), *Goethe; a collection of critical essays*, Prentice-Hall (Englewood Cliffs), 1984, p 152.

7. Goethe in *Maximen v. Reflexionen* (Stuttgart) 1943, p 536; quoted in Wilkinson, op cit, p 126.

8. Johann Wolfgang von Goethe, *Italian Journey*.

9. William Taylor Coleridge in Wilkinson, op cit, p 121.

10. Johann Wolfgang von Goethe in Wilkinson, ibid.

11. Goethe in a letter to Frau Stein, quoted in Leonard Willoughby, 'Unity and Continuity in Goethe' in 'Goethe's Conception of Form', Wilkinson, ibid, p 165. Willoughby discusses the issue of subjectivity at length.

12. Hartner, op cit, p 148.

13. Charles Darwin credits Goethe in *The Origin of the Species*, Bantam (New York) 1999, p 124.

14. Charles Darwin credits Malthus in *The Origin of the Species*, ibid, p 55.

15. Darwin, ibid, p 54.

16. Darwin, ibid, pp 66, 109, 400.

17. Georg Friedrich Hegel, trans Henry Paolucci, *Essays: On the arts*, Frederick Ungar (New York), 1979, p 4.

18. Ibid, p 11.

19. John Rosenberg (ed), *The Genius of John Ruskin: Selections from his writings*, Houghton Mifflin (Boston), 1963, p 178.

20. Richard Rorty, 'Dewey: between Hegel and Darwin', *Truth and Progress: Philosophical papers*, vol 3, Cambridge University Press, 1998, pp 83–128. Rorty is referring to James Kloppenberg, 'The Marriage of Darwin and Hegel', *Uncertain Victory*, Oxford University Press (New York), 1985, where Kloppenburg makes the original argument.

21. Oliver Wendell Homes, from *The Common Law*; quoted by Louis Menand (ed), *Pragmatism: A reader*, Vintage (New York), 1997, p xxi.

22. John Dewey, 'Experience, Nature and Art' in Louis Menand (ed), *Pragmatism: A reader*, ibid, p 249.

23. John Dewey, 'What I Believe' in John Patrick Diggins, 'Pragmatism and its Limits' in Morris Dickstein (ed), *The Revival of Pragmatism: New essays on social thought, law and culture*, Duke University Press (Durham NC), 1998, p 217, a discussion of Dewey's Futurism.

24. John Dewey, *Individualism Old and New*, Prometheus Books (Amherst, New York),1999, p 81.

Deborah Gans

25. Richard Bernstein, 'Community in the Pragmatic Tradition' in Morris Dickstein, (ed), *The Revival of Pragmatism: New essays on social thought, law and culture*, Duke University Press (Durham NC), 1998, p 148. Here Bernstein refers to Arendt's term in describing the Deweyian context of democracy.

26. Louis Menand (ed), *Pragmatism: A reader*, Vintage (New York), 1997 p xxviii.

27. Dewey, *Individualism Old and New*, op cit, p 43.

28. William James, quoted in Hilary Putnam, *Pragmatism: An open question*, Blackwell (Oxford), 1995, p 16.

29. Frank Lloyd Wright, *The Natural House*, Meridian (New York), 1954, p 40.

30. Frank Lloyd Wright, ibid, p 38.

31. Frank Lloyd Wright, ibid, p 181.

32. Richard Rorty, *Truth and Progress: Philosophical papers*, vol. 3 Cambridge University Press, 1998, p 301.

33. Rorty, ibid, p 316.

34. Ludwig Wittgenstein, quoted in Hilary Putnam, *Pragmatism: an Open Question*, Blackwell (Oxford) 1995 p 64.

35. Goethe, quoted by Wittgenstein in David Luban, 'What's Pragmatic About Legal Pragmatism' in Morris Dickstein (ed), *The Revival of Pragmatism: New essays on social thought, law and culture*, Duke University Press (Durham NC), 1998, p 288.

36. John Dewey, 'I Believe' in Louis Menand (ed), *Pragmatism: A reader*, Vintage (New York), 1997, p 267. 'Everything is so big that he [the empty individual] wants to ally himself with bigness and he is told he must make his choice between big industry and finance and the big political state.'

37. Rem Koolhaas, *S,M,L,XL*, Monacelli (New York), 1994, p 502.

38. Gottfried Semper, trans Henry Mallgrave, *The Four Elements of Architecture and Other Essays*, Cambridge University Press (Cambridge), 1985, pp 217–21.

39. See Gilles Deleuze and Felix Guatarri, trans Brian Massumi, *A Thousand Plateaus*, University of Minnesota Press (Minneapolis),1987, pp 440–7, passim.

40. Jean Baudrillard, 'The Ecstasy of Communication' in Hal Foster (ed), *The Anti-Aesthetic*, Bay Press (Seattle), 1983, pp 126–34.

41. Ben van Berkel and Caroline Bos, 'Radiant Synthetic Effects' in Cynthia Davidson (ed), *Anything*, MIT Press (Cambridge, Mass), 2001, p 12.

42. See such books as Mark Buchanan, *Nexus: Small worlds and the groundbreaking science of networks*, Norton (New York), 2002, pp 80–7, passim; and Kevin Kelly, *Out of Control: The new biology of machines, social systems and the economic world*, Perseus (Cambridge, Mass), 1994, p 22, passim.

43. Richard Rogers, *Cities for a Small Planet*, Westview (Boulder), 1994, pp 169–70, *passim*.

44. Chantal Mouffe (ed), *Deconstruction and Pragmatism*, Routledge (London), 1996, pp 6–7. Mouffe suggests that Rorty's and John Dewey's understanding of social process is limited because it assumes that conflict must and can be resolved through economic growth and development. She proposes another model that allows for the unresolvability and presence of conflict, and which does not demand unlimited tolerance as a basis for pluralism.

Zehra Kuz

Provocation

'Reason is the first principle of all human work.'

Thomas Aquinas

An analysis of the status quo reveals an undeniable rupture (not conflict) between thinking and making architecture. The physiognomy of the new space does not appropriate the building technology at hand. Reason, a planning tool, is submerged and the reality of space equals banality. Simultaneously, we have evidence that architecture as space is evolving and that architecture as a profession/trade is reforming. Truly interested in the transition, we will attempt to discuss the potential and possible paths from past to the future, in order to understand the motive of the transformation and the capacity of its effects on the environment.

A ripple effect followed from the emergence of electronic technology. The new tools entered architectural discipline through the world of production and later invaded the realm of operation. Moulding was added to the traditional methods of making architecture through carving and assembling. The positive impact of technical production enabled the realisation of milestone architectural masterworks.

After a brief gestation period, the proliferation of electronic technologies provoked an unprecedented acceleration in transfiguring architectural space. Loss of concrete form gave way to multiple formations. Planning, previously a wilful act of the architect, became an integrated feature of the computer program. Architecture is in a state of paralysis, suspended between the urging of form as (an individual) means of expression and lack of control over it.

In thought, this shift first emerged during the 1920s in the office of Mies van der Rohe, where Hugo Häring shared space after moving to Berlin. Their strong personal friendship allowed them to cultivate a conversation about controversial ideas of the Modern Movement, namely *formwollen* versus *formfinden*, German expressions that describe processes of arriving at a form. *Formwollen*, originally used by the art historian Alois Riegl to assess form as an absolute expression of pure will without consideration of its performance or function, suited Mies' position. *Formfinden* is used by Hugo Häring to describe his own new approach towards architecture. As Mies appropriated the idea of pure form as generic form for any function and any site, Häring computed/derived an idiosyncratic form based on variable factors such as site, user, programme, culture, etc.

Häring's approach to architecture was based on his own theories and writings, which were published under the title *Das Andere Bauen* (*The other way of building*). He differentiates between the form of purpose/performance and the form of pure expression. He writes: 'In nature, the gestalt of a thing is the result of an order of multiple elements in space, respective to their own unfolding life and performance and that of the totality.'[1] According to Häring, the form of purpose finds its shape naturally; its gestalt is the manifestation of its performance. In contrast, the form of expression depends on the psychological use of geometry in order to describe/manifest the gestalt. In the first case, the geometry is a means to an end, a vehicle; in the other, geometry is the motive itself.

Here I would like to quote a recent interview with Frei Otto, which was published in *Arch+* magazine. Asked to comment on the resistance and harsh criticism to his work during the 1950s, a rather conservative period in Germany, Frei replied: 'For the first time during the mid-fifties, modernism was introduced through Scharoun and Eiermann. Slowly the model of "let-it-develop" began to prevail as an anti-stylish building method vis à vis the right-wing extremist classicism.'[2] He then talks about his visit to the USA as a student on a scholarship:

> The Modern Movement did not come back as an ethical approach as we students hoped for, but as a messenger of form. I found the old German pioneers living in the USA rather unhappy. Although they were famous and extremely successful, they felt themselves misunderstood as the inventors of form. That was not the intent, especially for Gropius. The motto of the twenties was, 'We are not making a new style, we are making the new architecture/the mode of building (*Bauen*)'.

According to Otto, the guiding principle of the 1920s was misunderstood by its pivotal supporters, especially Philip Johnson. The main intent of the German core of the Modern Movement was to let form develop (*entwickeln*) itself rather than designing (*entwerfen*) it.

The interview continued with an inevitable comment: 'Your train of thought, that of "let it develop" eliminates the (artistic) architects . . .' Otto's response suggested the complexity of the situation and certainly reinforced the status of reason and structure in architecture along the lines of Häring's theories. He replied that 'the architect stays' and then set forth how the basic understanding of the terms 'natural' and 'artificial' had changed and how they belonged to different areas but were not oppositional. According to him, the new model of thought influenced art but not architecture. He concluded:

> The architects remained traditional, even when they invented new forms. They remained true to the conventions of planning. 'It will be built as I planned it.' As a result, for example, in the industry for tensile structures for stadiums, the clients now go directly to production companies; they bypass the architect. The manufacturers are capable of completing and delivering huge structures. During the last 15 years (now 18) the stadiums in Atlanta, Bari, Milan, Turin, Stuttgart are examples of such production. It is already happening to such a perfection that the architect is in fact superfluous in this process and this trend will penetrate into other areas.

Häring's responsive approach and Otto's 'let it develop' attitude towards architecture imply that the form is inherent in the specific task. Instead of superimposing form, the architect's responsibility is to let the form unfold and mature. Naturally, as such attitudes and trains of thought replace dogmas and methods, a number of questions emerge regarding the future of architecture as a discipline and practice. Planning conventions of a pragmatic nature are superseded by an array of newly assessed, idiosyncratic, undetermined factors, which are cultural, ideological, political, psychological and physical in nature. These, according to their relevance to the specific task, contribute towards the mutation of the built environment and human surround.

In the context of the multifaceted cultural revolution during the early 20th century, Häring's ideas represent an alternative approach to the mainstream architectural tendencies. The emerging ideas for modern living, although dramatically varied, uniformly desired change. The increased socioeconomic power of individuals led to the pursuit of idiosyncratic formal investigations. The ideals of democracy were manifested in transparency – literal and metaphorical. The social crisis that was a by-product of industrialisation resulted in the ideal of a holistic cultural vision. The formlessness in architectural space emerged in response to the concurrent sociopolitical change and as a criticism of the power of authority.

The organic, not as imitative of nature but as analogous to it, constituting a whole whose parts are mutually dependent or intrinsically related – an approach disqualified in the early 20th century – may in fact be terribly appropriate now. The inherent meaning, the complexity and the historical application of the term have the potential to relate to the current/contemporary cultural

Zehra Kuz

wilderness. With the promise of environmental symbiosis, the ideas of the organic are re-emerging in the concurrent context of ecology, infrastructure, and electronic technologies of perception and communication. The pressures of industrialisation and urbanisation are inspiring practitioners and theorists to juxtapose culture and nature and invoke organic terminology. The production of space for the current culture is the context for contemporary intertwined issues of technology and production, science and perception, and cultural conflict. The organic approach, as a mode rather than a model, as a programme rather than a form, was the theme of the conference.

The conference was configured in a series of interdisciplinary sections, each with a focus on a related subject. The renowned panellists, namely Günter Behnisch, Tom Brigham, Todd Dalland, Kenneth Frampton, Deborah Gans, Volker Giencke, John Johansen, William Katavolos, Haresh Lalvani, Ahmet Omurtag, Eeva Pelkonen and Mahadev Raman, came from the fields of architecture, engineering, mathematics, computer graphics, biology and critical theory to share their investigations related to the subject, especially matters involving architecture.

The first symposium was concerned with understanding the term 'organic' within its natural setting over a period of time relevant to our investigation, and establishing the scope of its use in the history of the culture of architecture. The Goethean, moreover the Hegelean, description of the organic is:

> Organic existence is this absolutely fluid condition wherein determinateness, which would only put it in relation to an other, is dissolved. Inorganic things involve determinateness in their very essence; and on that account a thing realizes the completeness of the moments of the notion only along with another thing, and hence gets lost when it enters the dialectic movement. In the case of an organic being, on the other hand, all determinate characteristics, by means of which it is palpable to another, are held under the control of the simple organic unity; none of them comes forward as essential and capable of detaching itself from the rest and relating itself to an other being. What is organic, therefore, preserves itself in its very relation.[3]

This quotation of Hegel evokes the dynamic spatial configuration which inspired the discussion.

Historical roots of formlessness in architecture and urbanism were reviewed to better understand the current deformations of architectural space, and a line of descent was traced from pan-German and Nordic traditions (namely Hugo Häring and Alvar Aalto). The panel explored the effects of the technological revolution of the past century, the consequent crisis of the city and the reassessment of nature in the Romantic Movement in the expectation of apprehending contemporary fluid space.

While the first symposium explored the empathic transfiguration of architectural space the second focused on tectonic ideas. The panel addressed the will to form from the inside, as compared to external factors and forces that come from the site and programme conditioning the object. The so-called organic transformation was reviewed on genetic, molecular, material and formal levels. In the need to develop an understanding of the impact of positive sciences in the formation of the 'gestalt' throughout the various levels of architectural processes, technologies were discussed as generators of form by material, structural, environmental and digital means. Questions concerning buildings, which are complex organisms developed to self-sustain their physical environments, were raised with regard to levels of exchange with their surroundings.

The third and final symposium viewed the organic as a context that involves urbanism and landscape, nature and culture, and socioeconomic factors. The investigation focused on continuity versus the boundary, within the existing definitions of a city and, in a broader sense, their relevance to the locale. Ultimately, the primary definition of 'organism' as an entity/existence that is only defined by its exchange of substances with the environment was challenged vis-à-vis the organisation of the built environment in connection with cultural and ideological manifestations and scale/limit.

The conference was organised to search for critical tools through which the progress in the evolution of spatial perception and production can be understood. It remains to be seen whether the organic approach will act as a catalyst of change.

Notes

1. Hugo Häring, *Das Andere Bauen*, Jurgen Joedicke (ed), Karl Kramer (Stuttgart), 1982, p 7.
2. This and other quotations from an interview with Frei Otto appeared in *Arch+* (1995).
3. GWF Hegel, 'Observation of Organic Nature' in *The Phenomenology of Mind*, Harper and Row (New York), 1967, pp 293–4.

Zehra Kuz

Part I

Evolution

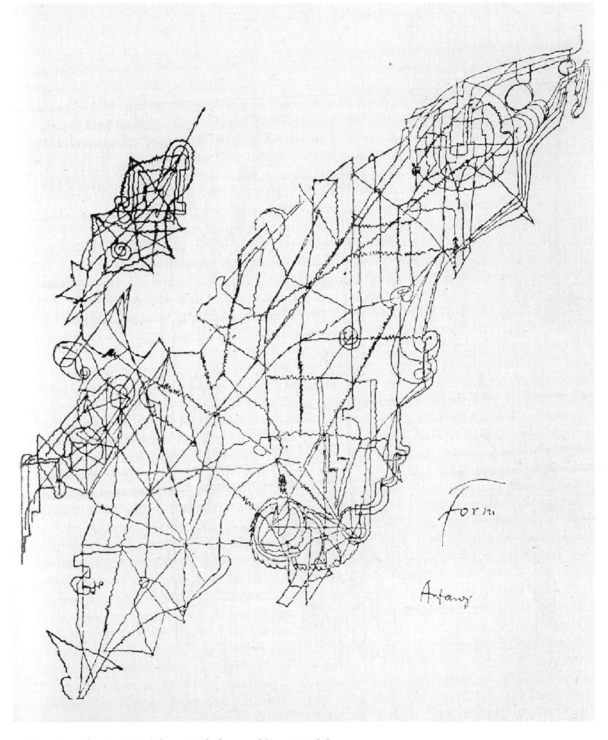

Anfang (transl. Beginning) from *Frülicht*, a publication of the
Glass Chain Group

1

Günter Behnisch

Work

At Behnisch & Partners the result of our work is the end of our endeavours. And that result is not necessarily what we intended at the beginning – or what we might have imagined at some intermediate stage. We change. The way we see things changes too. And our architecture changes: it changes in the course of our work, and as a consequence of it.

An example is the restaurant in the German Federal Parliament complex – the Bundestag – in Bonn[1] (1991), which is hemmed in by three other buildings. One of its sides gives on to the park and the Rhine, and its height is limited by the windows of the adjoining building. It is a 'shoe box' – low and long.

Some architects have a tendency to aestheticise the constraints inherent in a task. In this case, such architects might have focused on and poetically emphasised the cave-like, rather gloomy quality of the setting. Well, we take a different approach. We tend to reduce constraints and to highlight the freedoms that are also inherent in a task in reality; and, if it isn't possible in reality, we resort to 'magic'.

A young architect in our practice had been working on the restaurant for a long time. But somehow we weren't making any progress. The carcass was finished, but we still didn't know what our 'destination' was. Because of the low concrete ceiling slab and the building's proportions – dictated by the location – the interior was not unlike a bunker. We didn't like that. Bunkers are constructions in which a lot of violence has been invested; constructions associated with a very high level of fear. How were we going to cope with that?

1.
**Restaurant in
Plenary Complex of
German Bundestag,
Bonn, 1992**

Photo credit:
Christian Kandzia

What we felt was that sitting in a restaurant – at this place – should be like sitting outdoors in a park, in the light, beneath a green canopy of big old trees. So how were we going to go about it? We asked the painter Nicola de Maria, of Turin, to help us; we asked him to transform the problematic ceiling of the restaurant into a leafy canopy. We had a pretty clear idea of what we wanted. In southern Germany there are quite a few Baroque churches, palaces and castles. Because no other architectural solution was possible their enclosed inner rooms, which were inevitable at the time, were opened up by creating illusions with colours, sculptures, pictures, mirrors and so forth.

Nicola de Maria thought he could do something like that too. And, for several weeks, he painted. However, the final result was no leafy canopy, but a Nicola de Maria creation. **(Figure 1)** Surprising, and good. It dominated the room. Something we wouldn't have achieved without him. And we wouldn't have been able to imagine it in advance, either.

The simple fact is that things evolve; and we also evolve.

The world we know *today* will be a *different* world tomorrow.

And I think that with this insight we can approach our work in a relaxed way.

What I mean is that we should not finalise, and lock, our solutions to tasks too early. We should remain open, receptive to developments that we cannot know about in advance and to influences from areas that obey neither our will nor our logic. Also, if possible, we should not use planning methods that exclude influences that are not clear to us to begin with. Nor should we exclude forces of the kind that come from uncontrolled areas.

Nicola de Maria's painting, for instance, shows the importance, the value, of nonrationally planned elements in an overall work. We should keep our architecture receptive to elements of this kind. Sooner or later, of course, we have to make up our minds. But we try to postpone the moment for as long as we can – not always to the joy of our clients. We know from experience that what we design 'as a first step' will not be what is ultimately built. Why should we put shackles on our work in its early stages?

Perhaps the point we start at isn't all that important. What is important is simply to start. If we work well the result will be good. In trying to resolve problems we see what might work; and the better solutions come to us almost incidentally. And if we can't manage on our own we ask others for help: for instance, the artists Nicola de Maria or Erich Wiesner. The 'free arts' are an obvious choice because they can get to areas that we cannot reach by architectural means. The means available to architecture are less free; they are more closely bound to practical functions, to materials and technology and, of course, to physical laws.

In actual fact we are never finished; even when we have completed our work the results are always interim results. If we had been able to continue we would have arrived at different ones. This 'open' approach to design gives us new insights. Architecture evolves, continuously, and often in a way that surprises us.

The facts are:

- Our interests change. We are not always interested in the same things; our interests are repeatedly reoriented towards new factors inherent in a task – specific factors as well as general ones.
- Due to our own development, forces from various areas of reality influence us – forces that we are unaware of and do not recognise.
- Different people are involved.
- The possibilities a task offers are specific and different.

These facts – and many other elements – ultimately lead to the differences in the appearance of the buildings we design.

It was the case, for instance, that the Hysolar Institute Building at Stuttgart University (1990) was a 'quick' job – a building that was designed and built within a short space of time, although it had deep roots in the history of our practice. An experiment in form. **(Figures 2 and 3)** As to function, the problems were few. As to other issues, we asked:

Günter Behnisch

2.
Hysolar Research Institute, Stuttgart-Vaihingen, 1987

Photo credit:
Christian Kandzia

3.
Hysolar Research Institute, Stuttgart-Vaihingen, 1987. South façade showing layering of elements

Photo credit:
Christian Kandzia

4.
Hysolar Research Institute, Stuttgart-Vaihingen, 1987

- What are the options with regard to the organisation of form when we use large-dimensioned, industrially produced components; and
- How can we counteract the claims of technology, of technical apparatus and technical systems to create perfection – a claim we regard as inappropriate.

Designing a little schoolhouse in Bad Rappenau for children who, for whatever reasons, are maladjusted, we felt that in this special case the quality of weakness per se, and the weakness of these children, ought to be respected. In other words, we gave no illusion of power and perfection, nothing 'closed' but instead

Günter Behnisch

5.
Bus stop, Stuttgart
Feuerbach, 1991. View of
the linear with bomb
shelter in distance

a 'weak' kind of architecture of soft, craft-like constructions with a tendency to use natural materials. There was weakness in the formal sphere also. The building that resulted (1991) was of a kind we could easily have designed in the 1950s, at a time when our technological repertoire was still 'weak', when people in Germany were insecure and buildings wore a correspondingly weak appearance, with no trace of power-consciousness, and were in no way presumptuous.

For a bus stop at a bunker in the Feuerbach district of Stuttgart (1991) we focused on the contrast between the fearsome bunker and an open architecture, but without impinging on the self-confidence of the bunker which, like all other bunkers in Germany's history, had taken on a great deal of importance. **(Figure 5)** For a school in Frankfurt (1994) the building shuts itself off from an urban freeway and opens out towards a riverside environment. And for Nuremberg airport, a relatively minor airport, the operators wanted its new control tower (1986) to be an appropriate symbol.

For a long time there has been a debate about whether architecture can liberate itself from the claims of power, for example, the power of geometry. And what architecture should be like if it does. For instance Hugo Häring (1885–1956), a southern German architect who did not design a great many buildings but wrote and lectured, saw buildings as organs of society in material form. He used the term 'organwerk', and the role of this organwerk was to represent the 'essence' of the organ of society – and no doubt also to give it expression.

In my lifetime I've had more than enough to do with power and presumption, and their consequences. And like others, I was receptive to ideas like Häring's, which lead to the idea of freedom and democracy. In the USA this

kind of concept can be seen in the words of, for instance, Horatio Greenough, Louis Sullivan and Frank Lloyd Wright.

Larger projects, involving many of our staff, can't be as formally unequivocal as smaller buildings. It takes longer to design a larger building, there are a lot of influences, and most of the staff members are committed and want to make personal contributions to the joint design. They also want the building to be to some extent a reflection of themselves.

Points to note are:

- We usually obtain our work via architectural competitions.
- We provide the full range of architectural services, as is customary in Germany, including project management on site.
- We collaborate and form liaisons with individual trades and individual construction companies, with no general contractor or anything like that.

This means we have a great influence on the building. Unfortunately, these conditions, which are very much in our favour, are currently changing.

We have young architects in our practice. They come straight from university, so they are almost 50 years younger than I am. And they bring with them *their* time, and the spirit of *their* age. Maybe we could instruct them to design buildings in accordance with our ideas. But we don't like to do that. So we have to choose a type of architecture that is open, and also open for the young architects in the practice – open for new discoveries, open for the new era; but also open for the experience and the insights that come with age.

Hierarchical structures are not very well developed in our practice. The way things proceed depends on a lot of factors – on the job itself, on the client, on our architects and so forth. Some prefer to work one way, others have a different approach. Why should we standardise the way people work? A type of architecture that tends to be open and free needs open and free work in the office.

Günter Behnisch

Of course, some people attach importance to a more rigid outer framework. That's something we can't offer. And people who have an 'inner order' have no need of a rigid outer framework, and can act freely. It's a point that was also made by Frank Lloyd Wright. And a certain proportion of chaos is simply part of the picture.

Larger projects are tackled in a different way to small ones. The initial phase may be relatively clear and simple as, for instance, in the case of the competition design for the Congress Centre at the Hanover Fair (1992) – a facility to accommodate several thousand people above the exhibition halls. It is on three large legs, in my opinion a solution appropriate for a technological trade fair. On the other hand, our design of a high-rise building for a bank in Stuttgart (2002) wasn't characterised primarily by the usual general problems of high-rise buildings, such as stability or production technologies, but by a complex response – to its urban surroundings, for instance. It is a high-rise building that has a friendly 'Hello' both for its neighbours and further afield.

We weren't able to continue either of these projects. They remained at the competition design stage. What might have become of them if we'd been able to take them further, if we'd had to confront them with the so-called hard realities! On the other hand, it is a fact that we have so far always managed to preserve the crucial features of our competition designs in the finished buildings.

I have already said that large buildings and those that extend over a long period of time have to be approached differently from small, 'quick' designs. A case in point is the plenary chamber complex of the German Bundestag in Bonn. **(Figures 8-10)** We worked on this project for almost 20 years and it involved many of the architects in our practice. (As a rule, architects don't stay with us for more than five years.)

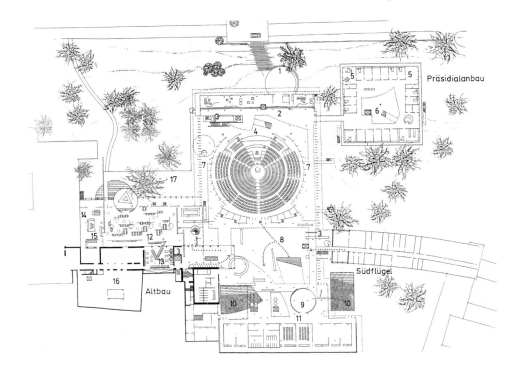

8.
Plenary Complex of German Bundestag, Bonn, 1992, Plan

**9.
Plenary Complex of
German Bundestag,
Bonn, 1992, View
into the Ambulatory**

Photo credit:
Christian Kandzia

**10.
Plenary Complex of
German Bundestag,
Bonn, 1992,
Entrance Hall**

Photo credit:
Christian Kandzia

Günter Behnisch

We try to make our work interesting. In every project we look for what seems to be special – if possible, something we have not previously discovered. On the other hand, the elements or qualities that are the same in every building soon lose their interest for us. We want special qualities to dominate rather than general, common features (although they also become part of the design).

We believe that every place, every object, every aspect, every moment in every job can be identified, and should develop of its own accord and be in its place. In this way, a society of fundamentally free, individual figures can come into being to make meshes and structures of localities and meanings, seemingly scattered at random in the architectural landscape – an order comparable to that created when a handful of pebbles is thrown into a pool. Craters are formed, large and small, and ripples that penetrate one another – both inside and outside the envelope of the building; a fundamentally free architectural landscape.

A staircase inside the building and a tree in the park may then be close to one another. A link is created between a foyer and a plaza, between an armchair and a bush, and so on. **(Figure 11)** The limits of the 'old' architecture, for instance, solid exterior walls, totally enclosed inner rooms, then cease to exist.

Interior and exterior are equal, have equal rights. It is true we have to build a glass outer skin, but we'd be happier if we could do without it. So we imagine that it's been eliminated. In the 'old' architecture, interior and exterior were important factors; but now, as distinguishing criteria, they're relatively weak.

In 1959, Martin Heidegger said: 'The limit is not where something ends; the limit is the point from which the essence of something begins.'[2]

However, we can go further. The next step aims at *not* harmonising the individual locations – the impact points of the pebbles – either in themselves, or in relation to one another, or in their position, or in their essence, or in the realm of form. One location or meaning may therefore be fully determined, another only sketchily; a third may be rectangular, a fourth oblique-angled; one location will be subject to problems of matter, another will be more immaterial.

And so forth.

Then, the material aspect of architecture disintegrates. The locations stand for themselves, and the relationships between these locations and meanings are immaterial. Where locations nevertheless merge materially, we regard it as a problem. Our task is to break up these agglomerations. And where it hasn't been possible in reality we have done it by 'magic'. In the case of the German Bundestag, for instance, by reflection, by mirrors, so that the individual locations appeared to be independent.

Even apparently individual locations will, of course, be related to the various strata of our reality. The one may be more strongly characterised by the material aspect and the laws of physics, while the other tends to be in the realm of biology. The third relates to one aspect of the job; and the fourth tends to be in the realm of fantasy, creativeness and so forth.

All this is possible. The component parts can be from different worlds, they can follow different pointers, and they can develop differently, according to

their natures. And this results in many layers, many networks of intermeshed relationships.

Architecture of this kind doesn't have to be harmonised from the outside. The free elements have their inherent order, and they group together – quasi-voluntarily – to form a new ensemble.

Naturally, we have to utilise construction materials and structures. And they, too, have their own orders, which they bring into the building. So there is something to be said for letting hard-working, load-bearing, structures spread the loads to which they're subjected *uniformly*. Geometric orders will easily result. However, it could be different . . .

The following constructions, at least, are not bound by the constraints of the load-bearing structure. They don't have to be compatible with the orders in the primary structure, and some components are, at least theoretically, completely free . . . like the lights in the lobby of the plenary chamber or the

Günter Behnisch

12.
Plenary Complex of German Bundestag, Bonn, 1992, 'bird's nest' railing in the foyer

Photo credit:
Christian Kandzia

railing in the foyer. **(Figure 12)** These elements operate in the practical sphere; but they also assume tasks of a different nature, for instance, symbolic tasks. Both reflect the principle of order. They establish priorities. The structure stands for rational orders. The lights or colours point to areas that cannot be commanded by rational means; and they point to their own orders, which at first we don't understand. And the railing also has the task of stabilising the curve of a balcony which turned out to be too weak.

Jan Mukarowski, a 'structuralist' from Prague, has written about problems of 'aesthetics'. Among other things, he notes that tangible objects or events which have little foundation in the practical-functional sphere gain importance in the realm of symbolism, where people seek reasons for why things are as they are.

Le Corbusier, for instance, subdivided the great glass partition in the refectory of the monastery of La Tourette into sections taken from a Gregorian choir. Even those who don't know this will suspect that a subdivision of this kind obeys concepts of order that are different to a division resulting from rational considerations. There are subdivisions of glass partitions which are intended to do nothing more than simply subdivide the glazed area into several smaller subsections – the kind of task that ought to be resolved rationally. But . . . there are also glass partitions that are present more by accident than design. And they are also left to chance – at least it appears that way – with regard to their subdivision. And there are elements that, as regards form, detach themselves still further from the demands of function – like the bench in the lobby.

I have already mentioned Hugo Häring, who wrote copiously on 'organic architecture'. In 1925, he wrote:

The things that we human beings create are the result of our endeavours in two directions; on the one hand we lay claim to the fulfilment of a purpose, and on the other to an expression. And so there is a conflict for form between claims of an objective, tangible nature and those of a spiritual nature; and matter supplies the means for this conflict . . .[3]

Elsewhere he wrote: '. . .the [fact] that things originate from demands of two types explains the entire mass of conflict . . . For it is obvious that the forms of the most suitable fulfilment of a purpose and the forms [created] for the sake of expression are not always congruent . . .'[4] Then: '. . . the forms of fulfilment of purpose . . . originate anonymously, so to speak . . . while the forms . . . for the sake of expression . . . are . . . subjective.'[5] And: 'The history of the judgement of the form of objects is . . . a history of the claims made on their expression.'[6]

Those were the convictions of Hugo Häring.

There are buildings in which many lines of development and many different points of view coincide. Such buildings – I believe that the German Bundestag building in Bonn is one of them – reflect many and complex energies and points of view; at least, for those who can and want to see these.

Although we designed the building, we repeatedly come across new aspects we weren't aware of at first. Evidently, in the course of developing the design, there were forces that were unknown to us. Gradually, we are coming to recognise them. Heiner Müller – a man of letters who died recently – when asked about this phenomenon, which also occurs in literature, said: 'The simple fact is that literature is wiser than men of letters.' Works of art can be reinterpreted repeatedly – in fact, ad infinitum.

The glossy ceiling reflects the light, and the green of the trees in the park surrounding the room. And thus the wide-spanned, and consequently strong and heavy, ceiling construction is 'enchanted'. As though we were outdoors, we see the green of the trees and of the lawn, we see the daylight and then the Rhine, too, the ships and barges moving up- and downriver, the opposite bank, people and seasons, and through the skylight we make out the sun, clouds, and rain.

Each of us sees what she or he can see and understands what he or she can. In architecture, I see a complex, deeply graduated system of sources of energy and relationships. As to how architecture was seen in the past, as an architecture of three-dimensional bodies and enclosed spaces, both interior and exterior – I have to force myself to see it that way. I believe that such a concept no longer corresponds to how we try to see and understand our world today. That way of seeing things belongs to a bygone age. And as we see things, so we think – and as we think, so we see architecture. And so we design, as well. We develop buildings layer by layer, as a rule working with specialists, each of whom is responsible for one layer. In order to work in this way we have to break the single entity down into separate areas. As I see it, we *would no longer be able* to work and think in any other way.

Günter Behnisch

Our practice is not specialised. We are pleased about every job we get, as long as it's interesting for us – schools, homes for the elderly, kindergartens, sports facilities and so on, be they large or small.

In recent years we have also designed some large administrative buildings, for instance for a public insurance organisation in Lübeck and a bank in Hanover. These are interesting jobs, it's true, but they're big, and they make big demands on the time and capacity of our practice. So we invest a lot – but the experience and the insights we gain concerning specifically architectural phenomena are no greater than those we get from a small project. Rather the contrary: the constraints and obligations inherent in large projects leave less freedom for architectural experiments.

Some problems that simply don't occur with small projects force their way into the foreground with large ones. For example, how can we prevent the individual from being engulfed by the mass? How can we see and address him or her as an individual? Buildings of this kind are marked by the struggle with size, on behalf of the individual.

We subdivided the large complex in Lübeck into smaller units, which we could assume would still be manageable by individuals. We assigned a wing of the building to each unit. And these wings are relatively independent. Each has its own subcentre, its own special outdoor area and its own colour(s) in the interior of the building. In the main lobby, at the centre of the complex, these units meet. We then emphasised problems in the formal aspects: the autonomy of the wings in the subcentres and their 'collision' in the central lobby. This results in formal 'vortices' in the lobby – a seeming 'muddle'. Of course, that gives us architects pleasure.

About 20 years ago we won a competition for a postal museum. The site was in Frankfurt, on the banks of the Main. There was an old villa, with a garden, and we thought we should design an equally autonomous, freestanding building – a solitaire like the villa – adjacent to it. While respecting the villa, our building could set itself clearly apart from the old one and its eclectic style through its modern technology, modern materials and the language of form of the 'modern age' among other things. So, on the one hand there would be the cuboid forms of the old villa, integrated in the forms of the roof; solid and punctuated with windows; built of sandstone, a craft-built construction inside and out, sparsely decorated with architectural details. And, in contrast, the long, slender new building, a skeleton construction made of reinforced concrete, light alloy and, naturally, with the formal order of the modern age. Some of the exhibition rooms had to be put under the garden of the villa. At this point the two buildings are linked to one another.

Julius Posener, an architect and writer on architecture who died recently, said, when he visited the building: 'My God, you've done everything the followers of the Modern Movement would have liked to do in the twenties, but for which, at the time, the necessary materials and constructions were unavailable.'

We don't hold the view that our buildings should all look alike, or at least similar. Nor does the market for architecture in Germany demand that we should deliver a kind of 'gallery architecture' ascribable to a particular artist-architect. We wouldn't like that, either. It is also true that our circumstances today are different from those of the architects of the 1920s. In those days they campaigned for modern architecture, formed groups and developed demonstrative projects. If we were to campaign in the same way today we would be 'kicking at open doors'. In my opinion the situation today is favourable for us. We can remain flexible and capable of responding.

Certainly, in Germany there were times when Post-Modern architecture was in vogue, and that put us under some pressure. And now, in Berlin, the so-called Rationalists are at work; and in Bavaria and Switzerland people are currently designing in the 'New Simplicity' style. Well, naturally, these waves come and go. They affect us only in so far as we assume them to be a reaction to shortcomings in everyday architecture. And we check whether our own architecture has shortcomings of this kind, and if necessary we correct ourselves.

The results of our work have many different faces:

In 1969, we won the architectural competition for the Olympic Park in Munich. The years around 1970 were special years in Germany. Our towns and cities, which had been destroyed in the Second World War had been rebuilt. There were new hospitals, new schools, new factories, etc. And the 'economic miracle' had been accomplished. A lot of people were satisfied with that. But there were others who felt that couldn't be all there was. It was the time when Willy Brandt said: 'Let us risk more democracy' – a time when the mood was one of 'a new beginning'.

The 1972 Olympic Games were associated with many hopes and aspirations. The Federal Republic wanted to present itself to the world as an open, liberal, youthful, athletic, artistic, innovative, democratic society. The wish was that the games should reflect these aspirations. And the architectural design was to be in accordance with this. It would be beyond the scope of this essay to describe our design in detail. But the jury was of the opinion that it came very close to fulfilling those wishes and aspirations. And it is a fact that the people did subsequently identify with this facility. Today, the Olympic Park is regarded as a monument of that social utopia of the years around 1970. According to surveys, the park is the most popular of Munich's attractions with the city's inhabitants.

This has given rise to problems. The city of Munich wants to alter the stadium in the Olympic Park. The soccer clubs that play there every week – for instance Bayern Munich – want the stadium facilities adapted to meet present-day requirements. Personally, I wouldn't have any objections to that. But voices are being raised against any such move.[7]

The Olympic Park is not far from the city centre. The site is about 2 1/2 kilometres long and 1 1/2 kilometres wide. After the Olympics it was to become a city park for the northern part of the city, which until then had remained underdeveloped. **(Figure 14)** A 'sculpted' architectural landscape was created where visitors and spectators move along the tops of the hills, embankments

14.
Olympic Park in Munich, 1969, General View

Photo credit: Christian Kandzia

etc, while the lower level is reserved for the sports events. The sports facilities are embedded in this sculpted landscape . . . more like hollows than buildings. The heavy concrete constructions that were needed are concealed below ground level. The landscape elements extend right up to the edges of the arenas, and visitors access the sports facilities from the top. So there are no 'buildings' in the conventional sense, with entrances, staircases, elevators and so on. And because we had no buildings, we couldn't build any roofs. But nevertheless we had to protect the facility from rain. And so, in collaboration with Frei Otto and Leonhard + Andrä, we developed a kind of 'giant umbrella'. The tent constructions for the German Pavilion in Montreal, on which Rolf Gutbrod also worked, were the precursors of the Olympic roof.

Ten years earlier, that is, around 1960, we had developed prefabrication systems of reinforced concrete – for instance, the one used for the *Fachhochschule,* or College of Technology, in Ulm, a building that is still good today. These systems were in accordance with contemporary requirements. People wanted to be able to occupy the buildings as quickly as possible. However, the systems, which comply with overriding concepts, also exercised real and formal constraints. And those constraints in turn had a backlash effect on our concept of

**15.
Olympic Park in
Munich, 1969,
Stadium**

Photo credit:
Christian Kandzia

19   Günter Behnisch

16.
Olympic Park in
Munich, 1969,
prestressed structure
of edge cables, nodal
fixings and wire
mesh

Photo credit:
Christian Kandzia

what architecture could be and could achieve. Before long we were no longer happy with the constraints. We wanted to be freer again – with our architecture, too. So we gave up the prefabricated systems and designed buildings that were influenced as little as possible by external constraints.

In Munich we had to set up a relatively large office quickly. We were joined by many – enthusiastic – employees. Given the circumstances we needed a 'working title' for the architecture we had been hired to create that would help us win the support of our new co-workers. We called it 'situational architecture' with the intention that the solution – functional, technological and formal – should be based on and developed from the specific situation, that preconceived formal concepts would not be accepted, that things should evolve from their own resources . . . and so on. We also found this concept in Sullivan, Wright, Gropius, Häring, and others – architects who had chosen 'organic architecture' as their working title. It was a wide-ranging concept that extended from a simple relationship to landscape, to nature, a mimesis of nature, to the open terminology of Häring. The arc extends from Sullivan's goal, to create form in accordance with 'the law of nature', to the design method of Gropius, who wanted a synthesis of art and technology, imagination and rationality. We had not formulated our approach all that precisely. Nonetheless, it helped us liberate ourselves from preordained forms and methods.

Given these approaches, the work on the landscaping, together with our friend Günter Grzimek, who died not long ago, was a real pleasure. And we had an equally easy time designing the sports facilities which were, of course, linked to the landscape. The roof construction was difficult – difficult in regard to the technology, the planning methods, the approval procedures, the deadlines and in regard to collaboration with others. And so, ultimately, the roof turned out more 'dogmatic' and 'stronger' than we had at first imagined.

But, as so often happens, the roof – the part we appreciated least – became the symbol of the Olympic Park and of the 1972 Olympic Games; in Germany it's in practically every sports programme on television. Just as, incidentally, there are hardly any news broadcasts that don't show footage of the plenary chamber of the German Bundestag in Bonn.

Allow me to add a few words on the relationship between theory and practice.

I began to practise architecture in the early 1950s, at a time when a lot had to be built in Germany, and built fast. Towns and cities destroyed in the war had to be rebuilt, and there were obsolete factories, hospitals, schools, etc to be replaced. Of course, there were architectural theories, such as the Modern Movement of the 1920s and early 1930s, and the Heimatstil theory from the same period. Both had quite deep roots. We read these theories, but didn't directly adopt them. We evolved our own theories in the course of our design and construction work, reflecting on our own practice, probably after the event. My own work was practice-oriented. What we designed was occasioned by needs, problems, habits and, certainly, also by general personal ideas. So our early buildings, around 1955, were influenced by 'nature-bound architecture'.

The prefabricated systems of the late 1950s were developed to allow more buildings to be produced, faster and of a better quality technically. Afterwards we tried to liberate ourselves from these generalised dictates. We wanted to work more openly, and also to deal with requirements from other areas. No doubt this happened around the time we were using the term 'situational architecture'.

As I have mentioned, our reflections on our work led to theories. These may have clarified our approaches. And they may also have influenced the buildings that followed. However, we wanted to remain as free as possible from powerful theoretical dictates. We felt that because theories reflect past events they are already dated when they are formulated. And they could easily become shackles or bonds, disrupting the living process.

I believe the forces that urge form into architecture are mainly pre-verbal. And when these forces are finally articulated verbally they lose a part of their original force and their vehemence. This problem could be recognised in buildings constructed in accordance with theories formulated by philosophers, which appear weak and Mannerist. Theories may provide a framework. However, artistic force also militates against that framework – that is, against the restrictions set up by theories. Nevertheless, I reflect on how it (framework, things) might develop, but without arriving at any conclusive result.

In Germany, the outward circumstances will change. Central and local governments, which up to now commissioned a lot of buildings, have less money than they used to. As clients they have practically dropped out. Their role has been taken over by investors or investment funds. Government departments had an on-the-spot political responsibility for their actions as clients – and also in education policy. Investors, on the other hand, appear to see their responsibility as being primarily for the invested capital. How could it be otherwise? They come from far away, possibly even from overseas, and don't have to answer on the spot for their actions. They will probably never again

Günter Behnisch

set eyes on what they have had built. By contrast, the balance sheets of their companies are very closed.

So . . . we are losing our old-style clients.

So far we have designed and built our buildings the conventional way – working with individual craftsmen and individual firms. Today, general contractors are elbowing their way on to the market and with them come project developers and project managers. Together with the investment funds, they form a legally united entity.

We could have managed without these companies, but now they're spreading in Germany like weeds in a garden. And the architecture created and managed by these organisations is coarser, more generalised, less dimensional. I don't think we can avoid this development in the long term. And there are already architects who are capable of playing this new game.

So far, however, our practice has occupied a different niche. We have designed and built more differentiated, and often also more detailed, buildings. The new organisational forms cause us problems. We are currently completing our first buildings in this new constellation; and we are trying to accept this new order, to overcome its constraints, and to emphasise the whole architecturally and poetically. We are attempting to develop a kind of architecture appropriate for these methods.

I am curious to see what comes of it.

Notes

1. The German Bundestag has moved to Berlin and the facilities in Bonn are now used for congresses, etc.
2. Martin Heidegger, *Poetry Language Thought*, trans Albert Hofstadter, Harper and Row (New York), 1971, p 83.
3. Hugo Häring, *Das Andere Bauen*, Jurgen Joedicke (ed), Karl Kramer (Stuttgart), 1962, p 45.
4. Ibid, p 87.
5. Ibid, p 17.
6. Ibid, p 47.
7. It has been decided that Munich will receive a new football stadium.

2

Zehra Kuz

Physiognomy of the New Architecture

Petrarca, an Augustinian monk, wrote a letter to his professor of theology in the year 1336. The letter, a confession, was a thorough description of an experience Petrarca had had just the day before, when he and his brother climbed the summit of Mount Ventoux, a mountain north of Avignon where the Rhône separates the French Alps from the hills of central France. It was not the first time that they had climbed the mountainous terrain but it was the first time they had challenged the summit. Upon his arrival at the highest point of the region, he became humbled by the sight and wrote:

> Shaken by the unparalleled winds from afar and the spectacle, I at first froze in fear. I looked: clouds beneath my feet. I turned my eyes towards Italy, to where my spirit drifted more than my eyes. I admit, I sighed as I saw the sky of Italy, which appeared to my soul rather than to my eyes, and an unexplainable longing overcame me to see my homeland again. At this very moment an idea emerged, which transposed me from space into time.[1]

He then continued describing the view to the west where he saw the mountains of the province of Lyon and to its left the Mediterranean and continued:

> Dismayed I was, I confess. As my brother asked my permission to read my writing, I shut my book. I was terrified that suddenly I cared for things of terrestrial nature. Instead I should have learned by now that

nothing other than the (holy) spirit is worth admiring, nothing would compare to her magnitude.[2]

According to Jean Gebser, an early 20th-century Polish-German philosopher and a thinker in many disciplines, Petrarca's letter is the manifestation of a new relationship between man and his spatial environment, which is also disclosed in the 14th-century frescoes of Ambrogio and the Lorenzetti brothers, and the paintings of Giotto, as an unprecedented space. Landscape replaced the flat, dark, red or golden background of the painting. This new recognition of the landscape led to a separation between the anima/self and the surrounding such as nature, which produced depth, the third dimension. The 15th century continued to witness the transformation of the European mind and the process of the spatial cognition. Perspective placed the observer and the observed at fixed points in space and focused the view on a specific sector.

Gebser developed a unique way of describing the evolution of human perception that manifests the characteristics of man's (inter) relation to his surroundings, social or spatial. According to his thesis, a cultural change/mutation takes place when the existing structure of consciousness cannot assimilate/internalise/comprehend (*bewältigen*) its own world. Apparently humanity has gone through five stages of consciousness during the course of cultural evolution – the archaic, the magical realm, the mythical, the mental and the perspectival – before reaching the a-perspectival stage. The archaic consciousness had zero dimension; the grasp of reality was based entirely on intuitive perception. There was no separation between earth and sky and inside and outside, instead there was a state of 'euphony'.

The magical realm, which is the next stage of this evolution, has the characteristic of one-dimensionality. During this period a focal point emerged which marked the centre within the human being. Although there was no speech mankind began to make tools, started to trade and was preoccupied with magical and natural powers.[3]

During the 'mythical' stage of the evolution the polarities of life and death, entrance and exit, being and absence were understood. The two-dimensional mental structure enabled speech, and the dialogue was born. Gebser thinks that this epoch (around 2000 BC), like dreams and childhood stories, is more accessible to our understanding today. The space during this epoch is described as nondirectional; the concept of depth, in other words distance, was not understood and nor was the measure of time.

The oracle of I Ching, Gebser argues, can be seen as marking the point of the evolution from the mythical to the 'mental' stage. The mental awakening transforms mankind's spatial perception, enabling human beings to grasp three-dimensional space. The triangle with two equal sides becomes the basis of the new logic and also implies the oneness of truth and one God. Evidently this is when the shift from matriarchy to patriarchy took place; Gebser compares this transition to the mental process which every teenager goes through during puberty. He argues that the 'mental era', which produced Euclidean geometry,

Aristotelian logic, Democritus' theory of the atom and Aristarch's heliocentrical system and perspectival space, is the foundation of our present culture, the 'integral era'.

Gebser observes that 'time' as a world constituent and perceived reality emerged from Einstein's theories on four-dimensional space-time continuums. The new consciousness became the setting for the spiritual transparency, diaphanousness, in which insight will replace knowing. According to him the new evidence is not a form of representation. It cannot be explained by methodical philosophy, but is understood through 'etiology'.[4] 'Philosophical thinking represents the world; however, integral perception of the world (through etiology) is pure evidence, hence truth. The byproduct which supports this statement is called "Systase".'[5] Gebser further explains that this expression describes the effect of all a-classified, a-categorical elements; so to speak all aspects of time which, because of its nonspatial character, could not become part of the classified systems. This all-integrating medium will be the catalyst to materialise and solidify spatial consciousness.

The shift from a 'perspectival' world to an 'a-perspectival' one is unclear unless we review the scientific discoveries of the 19th century. In the same way that Petrarca's letter, Giotto's paintings and the poems of the French troubadours catalyse the onset of the world of perspective, the discoveries of non-Euclidean geometry during the 19th century disclosed the a-perspectival world of today.

In his complete works, *Gesamtausgabe, Ursprung und Gegenwart, Zweiter Teil: Die Manifestationem des Geistigen* (Origin and present: The manifestations of the a-perspectival world, an attempt to materialise mind), Gebser supports his figure of thought (*Gebilde*) mathematically. According to him, 'a-perspectival' space is the manifestation of the space-time continuum and the fourth dimension. Euclidean geometry, a systematic body built by deductive reasoning, was founded on three main pillars and five postulates. For nearly 2000 years, scientists tried to prove that the fifth postulate, known as the 'parallel postulate', was a consequence of Euclid's other postulates. Gebser argues that the 19th century witnessed at least four separate, successful attempts within the same decade that proved, by constructing non-Euclidean geometry, that the fifth postulate was independent from the other postulates. Fr K Gauss (1777–1855) was the first to recognise that Euclid's fifth postulate implied more than three-dimensional space – the foundation of the non-Euclidean geometry. Shortly thereafter followed the proofs of the Germans Shweikart and his nephew Taurinus (1825), the Russian NJ Lobatschewskij (1829), the Hungarian J Bolyai (1832) and the German B Riemann. During his lectures on the psychophysical at the University of Graz (1864–5) Ernst Mach, without knowledge of Riemann's hypothesis, suggested an additional dimension regarding spatial perception. He referred to invisible phenomena, which were felt but not captured, as the action or labour factor. If one defined action by energy, one would obtain a time-related equation.[6]

Einstein developed his vision of n-dimensional space based on both a generic version of Riemann's concept and his own first theory of relativity (1905). Introducing time as the fourth dimension, he postulated a four-dimensional

Zehra Kuz

1.
Geschwister Scholl, Lünen, Westphalia, 1959–1962, Assembly Space, Hans Scharoun, architect
Photo credit: Mete Demiriz

space-time unit that became pivotal in explaining certain phenomena. Einstein's theorem is 'physiogeometrical' in nature, while Mach's is instead 'psychophysical'.

Gebser sets forth early that the title of Giedion's seminal work, *Space, Time, Architecture* shows a clear affinity to *Space, Time and Gravity*, A.S. Eddington's book on relativity theory. According to Gebser, Giedion recognised the impact of the new physics on perspective, in other words, the dissolution of perspective manifested in the Cubist paintings of Braque and Picasso, where the multiple lines of the drawings challenged more than just the gaze, bringing out the ambiguity of the subject matter. Their method of presentation implied the superimposition of several points of view, several moments of time, wherein the object and the space that contained it became transparent, allowing the drawing to become four-dimensional, hence a-perspectival.[7]

Gebser sees relativity theory as also directly related to architectural culture. He frequently refers to Frank Lloyd Wright's description of the new architecture, in which the measuring unit of time has become a new measuring unit of space, where all fixed relationships are replaced by flexible ones. The onset of the time factor as movement dissolves the rigid space into a fluid one, turning it into a space-time continuum. For Gebser, the incorporation of the fourth dimension is the evidence of a-perspectival space.

Similarly, Scharoun's 1956 competition entry for the Philharmonie, the hall for the Berlin Philharmonic Orchestra, overcomes the rigid organisation of one-point perspective masterfully. A diaphanous landscape manifests itself from inside and out. Although seemingly complex, the orientation and movement through the facility is self-evident. Planned around a hexagonal podium, the Berlin chamber music hall has an essentially triaxial arrangement that denies the convention of longitudinal and cross axes, increasing the sense of rotation. While the podium and the inner seating-terraces conform to 60-degree geometry, the periphery breaks away to a more complex arrangement. Deviation from the

rigid order not only emphasises the centrifugal dynamics of the space, it also improves the acoustics by deflecting and dispersing the sound reflection paths. In Scharoun's own words:

Music as the focal point: this was the keynote from the very beginning. This dominating thought not only gave shape to the auditorium of Berlin's new Philharmonie but also ensured its undisputed priority within the entire building scheme. The orchestra and conductor stand spatially and optically in the very middle and if this is not the mathematical centre, nonetheless they are completely enveloped by their audience. Here you will find no segregation of producers and consumers, but rather a community of listeners grouped around an orchestra in the most natural of all seating arrangements. Despite its size, the auditorium has retained a certain intimacy, enabling a direct and co-creative share in the production of music. Here the creation and the experience of music occur in a hall not motivated by formal aesthetics, but inspired by the very purpose it serves. Man, music and space come together in a new relationship.

The construction follows the pattern of a landscape, with the auditorium seen as a valley, the orchestra surrounded by a sprawling vineyard climbing the sides of its neighbouring hills. The ceiling, resembling a tent, encounters this landscape 'like a skyscape'. Convex in character, the tent-like ceiling is very much linked with the acoustics, with the desire to obtain the maximum diffusion of music via the convex surfaces. Here the sound is not reflected from the narrow side of a hall, but rises from the depth and centre, moving towards all sides, then descending and spreading evenly among the listeners below. Every effort was taken to transmit the sound waves to the most distant parts of the auditorium by the shortest possible route. The diffusion was also served by the reflection of the auditorium walls, and the multi-levelled, heterogeneous

Zehra Kuz

arrangement of the 'vineyard terraces' . . . Can it be an accident that wherever improvised music is heard people tend to gather around the performers in a circle? The psychological basis of this natural process seems self-evident to all; it had to be transposed into a concert hall.[8]

Scharoun' s design approach is quite clear; the gestalt of the Philharmonie is not the result of haphazard planning; instead it is the manifestation of a spatial consciousness interwoven with specific performance. An analog *modus operandi* is visible throughout his work. From the early 1930s until after the mid-1940s the groundwork of Scharoun's architectural *oeuvre* was the private house; this was the only kind of commission he had in the political climate of the time. Although the houses had to comply with the requirements imposed by the nationalist government, they successfully hid an explosive new spatial experience behind picturesque facades made of traditional materials.

Take, for example, the Baensch House built in a suburb of west Berlin in 1935 during the Nazi era, when tight restrictions were imposed by the building authorities. The plan is evidently the result of the particular places and shapes of different functions without any emphasis on any single one. The views and the orientation are appropriated for different activities. Space seems to flow in various directions through areas which are subtly defined by a change in level or material. A great lightness transpires from these rapid changes, which seem to happen in a haphazard way. The layout of the garden level, which seems to cascade along with topography, like a fan, does not correspond to the upper level for the bedrooms. The exterior, with exposed brick walls and pitched roof, artfully disguises the unconventional interior.

The best example of this period is the house (1936–7) for the painter Oskar Moll on the west bank of the Halensee, near Berlin. The bulk of the house is situated perpendicular to the northeast boundary of the site. A second perpendicular system is introduced, as in the staircase which is shifted 90 degrees to the southwest boundary. The staircase links nine interacting levels from the entrance level up; the living room, music room, dining room, large study, the garden and the upper-floor bedrooms. While the ridge of the roof follows the street, the stairs parallel the lake. A dynamic walk-through reveals an astounding spatial transfiguration, which starts from a conventional small entrance and continues via stairs to a multilevel, multipurpose room with a circular dining area on one side and a slightly sunken living area on the other. The second floor accommodates four bedrooms with a view towards the lake. The spatial experience is emphasised/magnified through the sectional development of the house, especially at the garden level. Some 15 years later Scharoun described his design intent as follows:

The Moll House was based not on a geometric principle but on a system of interconnections – in contrast to the many-roomed 'villa' in which the living spaces fulfil technical and economic requirements but are subordinate to financial and geometrical constraints. I will show you, using the example of the Moll House, that giving up the right angle and the free form is not an act of wilfullness, but a true response to the landscape and needs of the people.[9]

In fact, the study of Scharoun's design approach is not complete without the voice of Hugo Häring, the German architect who had developed theories on organic architecture. It is known that the two men had very strong ties. Scharoun, at least 15 years Häring's junior, was the more fluid designer. During the 1950s, when Germany was being rebuilt, he was young and strong enough to focus on a career, while Häring was unable to pursue his work because of ill-health. Häring's ideas and theories were echoed in Scharoun's work; Scharoun had the chance to test and materialise Häring's ideas on *'das andere bauen'* (the other way of building). The work of both men, Häring's theory and practice combined with Scharoun's architectural *oeuvre*, is pivotal to understanding the alternative approach to the modern concept.

In this particular instance, it is illuminating to quote Häring's words on 'Work on the Ground-Plan' (1952*)*:

> The set task is clear: the house must be laid out from the inside outward, starting with the life-processes of dwelling, and proceeding according to this principle. The exterior is no longer determined in advance, but arises in the same way as in all organic development. The exterior does of course set limits on this organic development, but does not dictate its form. One throws walls around processes of the dwelling, one does not force the dwelling processes into rectangles. Working this way, walls are hardly likely to end up at right angles, nor is one likely to end up with a rectangular building. Also the walls will not always end up straight. A natural order will assert itself, with the tendency for each part to find its appropriate relation with the sun, so that the house opens out towards the south and swings around from east to west, while it turns its back to the north. It behaves like a plant presenting its organs to the sun. We are in a general sense ready to bring the *'Organwerk'* of building into line with life, yet we have scarcely begun to take the next step, the development of *'Gestaltwerk'*. *'Gestaltwerk'* has a leading character. The spaces understand their serving role. They receive their gestalt from inhabitants and their dwelling habits; they belong to life and take part in it. They become being-like (*wesenhaft*), no longer following the abstract structure of another world of forms. This also applies to the materials from which the body of dwelling is constructed, which are chosen not for their technical performance alone but also for the quality of life and the experience offered when living with them. It strives for the same kind of harmony between building and dwelling that we admire in the tradition of the Japanese house, a tradition which never suffered suppression under the form of geometry.[10]

Parallel to Gebser's theories on the evolution of human perception, Häring developed his own theories that the culture of architecture evolved from a

Zehra Kuz

pregeometric to a geometric and, finally, to an organic phase/stage. For Häring, geometry and the organic are the two principles of form-(gestalt)-making and the forming forces of nature. The geometry is the ordering principle of the crystals, while the ordering principles which form the organisms are conditioned by the 'life task' of their organs. According to Häring the geometric era was coming to a close and the future had a chance to pursue the organic approach in regard to 'gestalten'- form-finding analog to nature. He points out that:

> Organ-like nature has her own form ideas, she makes organs that serve the fulfilment of a living process, she does not content herself with the abstract space arrangements of geometry. In this space arises a new concept of form-creation: the living as a changing process, no static state. It is moved and moving, not rigid and dead. It is bound up with the secrets of creative life, it runs according to the life-effecting secret energies of the spritual world.[11]

In German culture the term 'gestalt' is used in all topics concerning existence, especially in art history, biomorphology, mythology and theology. Goethe described the term 'Gestalt' (structured form) in his essay 'On Morphology' as the German word for the complex of existence presented by a physical organism:

> With this expression they exclude what is changeable and assume that an interrelated whole is identified, defined, and fixed in character. But if we look at these 'Gestalten', especially the organic ones, we will discover that nothing in them is permanent, nothing is at rest or defined – everything is in a flux of continual motion. This is why German frequently and fittingly makes use of the word 'Bildung' [formation] to describe the end product and what is in process of production as well.[12]

For Häring, the term 'gestalt' implies form imbued with meaning and refers to entities. According to him, gestalt is a structural concept of reality – it is sensory as well as mystical. He also draws parallels between organic structures and order within society, wherein the relationship of the individual to the community is directly compared to the relationship of the single cell to the organ. Once again Häring's ideas are masterfully manifested in Hans Scharoun's school projects during the 1950s and the early 1960s.

The Geschwister School in Lünen, Westphalia, was the first opportunity for Scharoun to apply his ideas, which he had developed earlier for a school project in Darmstadt (1951). The project for a primary school in Darmstadt was his contribution to the competition invitation by the city of Darmstadt under the title 'Mensch und Raum' (man and space). As well as a number of prominent architects there were also philosophers and sociologists on the list of the invited. Scharoun's proposal was ground-breaking for its pedagogical features as well as for its architectural formation. Although the Darmstadt school project was celebrated and widely published, it did not get built. The ideas, which

2.
Geschwister Scholl,
Lünen, Westphalia,
1956–62, Entry,
Hans Scharoun,
architect

Photo credit:
Mete Demiriz

3.
Geschwister Scholl,
Lünen, Westphalia,
1956–62, Roofscape,
Hans Scharoun,
architect

Photo credit:
Mete Demiriz

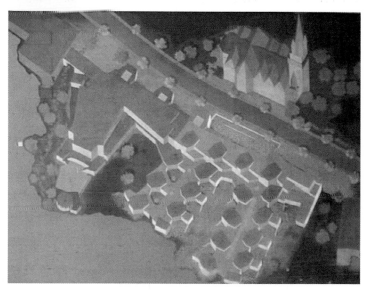

4.
Geschwister Scholl,
Lünen, Westphalia,
1956–62, colour plan
of the Aerial View,
Hans Scharoun,
architect

Photo credit:
Mete Demiriz

Zehra Kuz

5.
Above
Geschwister Scholl, Lünen, Westphalia, 1956–62, Stair Hall, Hans Scharoun, architect

Photo credit: Mete Demiriz

6.
Left
Geschwister Scholl, Lünen, Westphalia, 1956–62, Hallway, Hans Scharoun, architect

Photo credit: Mete Demiriz

7.
Geschwister Scholl, Lünen, Westphalia, 1956–62,
Hallway, Hans Scharoun, architect

Photo credit: Mete Demiriz

were developed together with his assistant Alfred Schinz who was well informed about the School Reform movement in Germany, were developed further for later school projects, which have been built. In fact, all of the three school projects Scharoun designed were fragmented, single-storey buildings, which were widely spread so that the building in its entirety could not be seen at once. Similar to urban spaces, all the projects were organised around internal streets and places; the streets led to a cluster of classrooms and the plazas gave way to the main activity areas such as the gym and assembly hall.

While the school in Lünen was built in phases, undergoing modifications to the original intent, the primary school in Marl, Westphalia, became an extraordinary example of theory and practice merging. The spatial organisation of the school, which was built on an open suburban site, displays a great emphasis on the concept of cityscape, as the form and the location of the assembly hall marks the school's focal point. The assembly hall and the gym were also made available for public use, in order to bring the daily life of the town into that of the school.

The classroom clusters are like neighbourhoods and are arranged according to the age groups of the children. Each cluster has a hallway, a 'so-called communal space', which leads into the classrooms. The passage between the hallway and the actual classroom goes through an extended threshold, like a bottleneck; it is a small lobby, which also holds the coat closet and the wet rooms. This zone, which is darker and much smaller than the classroom on the one hand and the corridor on the other, provides the children with the physical awareness of a spatial transition between play and work activities.

Classrooms are hexagonal and have a clerestory which lets daylight penetrate throughout the entire space. There is no prevailing order for the arrangement of classroom furniture. It is placed according to the teaching methods – a linear arrangement for straight teaching and a more circular layout for seminars. A small annex provides an intimate work space for smaller group activities and

Zehra Kuz

from it the teacher can supervise both areas – the classroom and the annex –
simultaneously. The location of the annex also forms a cove-like outdoor teaching area, the shape of which is manipulated according to the pupils' age group.
The older grades have privacy and closure to further concentration, while the
lower grades have more of an open space visually.

Scharoun explains his approach to his school projects:

> The most important task of education is the insertion of the individual
> into the community through the development of a sense of personal
> responsibility, in such a way that the community that results represents
> more than the sum total of individuals it contains. This aspect of educa-

11.
Primary School,
Marl, Westphalia,
1962, Entry,
Hans Scharoun,
architect

Photo credit:
Mete Demiriz

12.
Primary School,
Marl, Westphalia,
1962, Main entrance,
Hans Scharoun,
architect

Photo credit:
Mete Demiriz

tion cannot be thought directly, it is rather a matter of general experience and gradual formation of consciousness, which allows the individual to find the right contact with public life and with political community . . . Thus a school building should not be a symbol of power nor primarily a product of technical or artistic perfection. Like any other building, a school should communicate an idea of a way of life sympathetic to the universal principle of democracy.[13]

As you stroll through this man-made landscape an immensely rich spatial configuration unfolds, widening, narrowing and intertwining through various zones with different height and light intensities that otherwise can only be experienced in natural surroundings. These brightly coloured rooms or zones provide children with spatial identity and hence a sense of belonging. You can let yourself drift along the corridors and still arrive at your destination as if a

13.
Primary School,
Marl, Westphalia,
1962, Collective
space, main
entrance, upper
level, Hans
Scharoun, architect

Photo credit:
Mete Demiriz

built-in navigation system, operated by spatial topology, daylight, colour and material, is second nature to the building. From the entrance to the exit you are within a space-time continuum; once in the belly of the school you can still remember, in fact see or perceive, the threshold/door you entered through and the distant space you are heading towards; past, present and future collapse at once on to each other.

Whether the work of Häring–Scharoun was inspired by the theoretical output of pan-German culture as a critical response to industrialisation and the crisis emerging from it, by Scheerbart's vision of a utopia[14] that was home to a new culture based on democracy or by the concept of Functionalism as described by Greenough is not exactly known. Their work references concurrent philosophical and sociological ideas that were emerging. Theories about creating an organic community in order to restore the cultural rifts in a mobilised society and establish a balance between the concept of modern life and its reality, evidently became ingrained in their train of thought. In addition both men, inspired by 'gestalt psychology' – another German product at turn of the 20th century – and anthropology, refined their concept of design, experimenting with the human perception of space and the psychology of form. Their design approach selectively incorporated interdisciplinary ideas, beyond construction, beyond technology. Häring developed his theories intuitively and was well aware of Gebser's elaborate thinking and writing on a similar subject. The idea of an all-encompassing, a-perspectival space as discussed by Jean Gebser in his writings, which prognosticate an inevitable condition in the evolution of man's perception of space, emerged in Scharoun's architecture.

According to Gebser the era of absolutism and the totalitarian approach came to an end. The space-time continuum required a new structure, a new consciousness. To comprehend the integral perception of the (physical?) world, he

14.
Primary School,
Marl, Westphalia,
1962, Classroom,
Hans Scharoun,
architect

Photo credit:
Mete Demiriz

uses the term 'systase', which is 'accumulation and unification of parts to the whole', hence the integrating dimension. This mental concept discloses 'synaesthesia', which is described by Brian Massumi:

> Clinical synaesthesia is when a hinged dimension of experience, usually lost to active awareness in the sea-change to adulthood, retains the ability to manifest itself perceptually. In synaesthesia, other sense dimensions become visible, as when sounds are seen as colours. This is not vision as it is thought of cognitively. It is more like other-sense operations at the hinge with vision, registered from its point of view. Synaesthetic forms are dynamic. They are not mirrored in thought; they are literal perceptions. They are not reflected upon; they are experienced as events . . . Synaesthetic forms can be usefully recombined with an experience of movement. They serve as memory aids and orientation devices. Since they work by calling forth a real movement-experience, they retain a privileged connection to proprioception. This is not cue-based, form-and-configuration vision. Although synaesthetic forms are often called 'maps', they are less cartographic in the traditional sense than 'diagramatic' in the sense now entering architectural discourse. They are lived diagrams based on already lived experience. Lived and relived: 'biograms' might be a better word for them than diagrams.[15]

A walk through the physical space of Scharoun's architecture reminds one of such a concept. The physical experience is not a hallucination, but a reality that is hard to grasp. There is no point of photographic representation of this space; it is in a constant flux. The structure relies entirely on diaphanous human perception. One is navigated through space by an inner knowing. Perhaps the reality of this extremely delicate landscape may be the link to the current prevailing architectural culture. Häring would say:

Zehra Kuz

The things we human beings do are the result of our efforts of a dual nature; on one hand we require purposefulness on the other we demand expression. The prerogatives of the physical clash with the prerogatives of spiritual nature in the course of making a thing, while the material assumes the role of the mediator between the two objectives. However, how these prerogatives affect and condition the thing itself vary for every project due to its (own) time, the landscape it is part of, folks it belongs to and material it is made of.[16]

Notes

1. Jean Gebser, *Gesamtausgabe, Ursprung und Gegenwart, Zweiter Teil: Die Manifestationen der aperspectivischen Welt, Versuch einer Konkretion des Geistigen*, Novalis Verlag, 1986, pp 35–44.
2. Ibid.
3. According to Gebser's theories, in the beginning the idols of Eurasia and human representations by aborigines in Australia show no mouth; instead the only show ears.
4. Etiology: reason of being or ethology; the study of relationships between an organism and its environment.
5. Gebser, op cit, pp 35–44.
6. Ibid, pp 456–83.
7. Ibid, p 620.
8. Peter Blundell Jones *Hans Scharoun*, Phaidon (London), 1995, pp 178–9.
9. Ibid, p 94.
10. Peter Blundell Jones, *Hugo Häring*, Menges, 1999, p 160.
11. Ibid, p 185.
12. Douglas Miller (ed), *Goethe the Collected Works*, vol 12, Scientific Studies, Princeton University Press, 1995, p 63.
13. Peter Blundell Jones, op cit, p 136.
14. Scheerbart's 'Utopian Phantasmagoria' (1893) evokes the vision of a new architecture as a reflection of a new culture. Glass Architecture would be crystal clear, mobile and colourful, and would achieve a transparency and lightness that would transform old feelings, thoughts and habits. A decade later Scheerbart's ideas inspired an artists' movement that opposed the exclusively positivist tendency of the contemporary culture. New creations of the industrial civilisation resulted in new conventional customs and a bourgeoisie. Strongly supported by publications such as *Der Sturm* and *Die Aktion*, the group criticised materialism, militarism and nationalism. Realism and naturalism were replaced by fragmentation and distortion. Syntactic elements in poems and paintings were abandoned in order to defy empirical reality . . . The architecture of activism was born in this era and headed by Bruno Taut. The ripple effects of the Glass Chain movement continued throughout the years after the First World War. The extent and the influence of the movement is manifested in the entries for a competition on Friedrichstrasse, Berlin, in 1922: the Taut brothers, Mies van der Rohe, Häring, Mendelsohn, Poelzig, Hilberseimer, Behrendt, etc.
15. Brian Massumi, 'Strange Horizon: Buildings, biograms and the body topologic', *Hypersurface Architecture II, Architectural Design*, vol. 69, no 9–10, p 12.
16. Hugo Häring, 1925.

3

Eeva Pelkonen

Transitions:
Alvar Aalto's Approach to Organicism

In autumn 1930 Aino and Alvar Aalto designed a 60-square-metre dwelling furnished with prototypical upholstered chrome tube furniture for the Minimum Apartment Exhibition, which they coordinated at the Helsinki Konsthallen.[1] In 'Our Apartments as Problems', an essay in *Domus* (1930), Aalto introduced the concept 'biodynamism' to describe the design concept based on the fluid occupation of space: 'A home is an area that forms a sheltered space for eating, sleeping, working, and playing. These biodynamic forms must serve as the basis for the internal divisions of a home, not obsolete symmetrical axes and standard rooms dictated by façade architecture.'[2]

In order to illustrate his flexible approach to function, Aalto distinguished between *huone* (a regular room pertaining to a single function: kitchen, bedroom, etc) and *tupa*, a large multifunctional room found in traditional, particularly Carelian farmhouses. Since both are rectangular the difference, he argued, was not formal but, rather, structural. The first model compartmentalised functions into separate spatial units, the latter allowed different daily activities – cooking, working and sleeping – to unfold 'organically' in a large nonprogrammatic space. A logistical coordination allowed different functions to take place at different times. For example, a living room can double as a bedroom. In other words Aalto's biodynamism referred to the structural and logistical coordination of various functional scenarios within a single space. He considered easy shifts from one function to another equally crucial for modern man: 'One might say that an apartment in which moving about, the transition from one task to another, can take place organically – without difficulty or disturbance – and

1.
**Alvar Aalto's
Minimum Apartment
Exhibit, 1930**

Photo credit: Alvar
Aalto Archives,
Helsinki

which has advanced insulation, internal acoustics, correct distribution of light, etc. already confers a high degree of comfort.'[3]

Aalto's notion of 'biodynamism' can be traced to two concepts used by Laszlo Moholy-Nagy (1895–1946), the Hungarian-born Bauhaus teacher and multifaceted artist, who could be singled out as Aalto's soulmate and strongest intellectual and artistic influence between 1930 and 1932. In the chapter 'Biotechnique as a Method for Creative Enterprise' in his *From Materials to Architecture* (1929), Moholy refers to naturalist Raoul France's concept of 'biotechnics', that is, that all life is based on necessity and the preservation of energy.[4] In an earlier book, *Painting, Photography, Film*, he had talked about the ability of camera and film to capture the dynamism and tempo of modern life.[5] The original title of *From Materials to Architecture – From Art to Life* – captured the moral dictum behind the concept: art's function was to help every man live life to its fullest potential, to 'produce' life rather than merely represent it.

In the Minimum Apartment article, Aalto too used the concept of 'life' as a theoretical umbrella in order to define the larger moral and ethical maxims of Modernism:

> By starting out with the minimum apartment and adding constantly to its potential so as to enlarge it psychologically, we arrive at the concept that is no longer a minimum apartment but a general-purpose apartment – with better and more appropriate qualities than an apartment in which an emotionally based treatment of size has led to an unorganic result.[6]

Aalto's proposal for the minimum apartment can be understood as a commentary on those proposed at the 1929 CIAM conference at Frankfurt: the design was not the mere fulfilment of functional requirements but rather an apparatus through which man realises himself through space. Indeed, the project was conceived as a critique of the minimum apartment concept. Yet, rather than rejecting Modernism altogether, the idea here was that a spatiotemporal experience provides a microcosm which enhances the continuum between individual experience and processes of modernisation.

Aalto's idea of 'biodynamic' and 'organic' occupation of space was analogous to Oskar Schlemmer's idea in *The Stages in Bauhaus* of how man occupies and creates space.[7] According to Schlemmer this interaction was based not on visual experience alone, but on the interweaving of man as a complete physiological entity with space through movement. In his essay Schlemmer wrote:

> The lawfulness of an organic man is based in the invisible functions of
> his internal organs: heartbeat, breathing, brain functions and nerve
> system. These functions define the centre of the human being, whose

Eeva Pelkonen

movements and radiance define an imaginary room. The cubist-abstract space is therefore only a horizontal-vertical support system for this fluid condition. These movements are organic and based on feeling.[8]

The pictures accompanying Schlemmer's article defined the relationship between man and space in three stages: the first picture depicts a figure in a cubic space mapped out with horizontal, vertical and diagonal lines. In the second image, the lines map the curvilinear movement of arms and legs. In the third diagram, the two networks form a kind of interlaced system, where the internal system and the external spatial conditions overlap. Schlemmer's model of spatial organisation was continuous with the nervous system, blood circulation etc. In other words, man exists within and through space. This suggests that space could become a tool for managing human activity and behaviour. 'Every individual represents an energy reserve; mismanaging this reserve is the greatest possible diseconomy for society', wrote Aalto, implying a subtle balance between individual freedom and societal control.[9]

Moholy also taught Aalto to express the complex cultural phenomena called modernity with new representational means (photography, abstraction), new design methods (experimentation, organisational strategies) and some key ideas in German architectural theory such as biodynamism and, indeed, organicism. Aalto's quick adaptations of Moholy's trademark photographic techniques – oblique angles, spatial layering and aerial views – demonstrate how he started at this time to understand modernity not only as a socioeconomic construction but also as a particular experience of time and space. Indeed, the lesson learnt from *From Material to Architecture* was that all scales of the natural world are governed by the same principles, and that the same should be true for a man-made environment. A close-up of the wrinkles on an old man's face would suddenly correspond to those on the earth's crust.

The principle of dynamic transformation of scale was most commonly used in urban and regional planning where it was considered a prerequisite for a modern industrialised society to come into being. In *Acceptera*, the group of Swedish architects involved in the Stockholm Exhibition of 1930 – Sven Markelius, Gregor Paulsson, Eskil Sundahl and Uno Åhren – distinguished between the city as a 'living organism' and the city as a 'work of art' as follows:

> A city as a work of art is a dangerous concept. [A city] is not something permanently static like a sculpture or a painting. It is a result of real needs, whose changing nature should be taken into consideration. A city is an expression of movement, work, life of a thousand different kinds. It is a living organism . . . The environment is and must be a changing entity.[10]

They further expand the notion of organic planning to an even larger scale that encompasses all of Europe. In a chapter titled 'Cultural situation. A- and B-Europe' the authors defined the terms: 'A-Europe is like a big "organism", where all functions are at once specialised and centralised, and where all cells from small gardens to the big factories and banks are dependent on one another.'[11] 'A-Europe' was immersed in the processes of a modernisation connected by infrastructural networks such as railroads, whereas 'B-Europe' was isolated, hence unorganic, and did not therefore participate in economic progress. Organicism became a metaphor for a world that had become increasingly international and interconnected.

Aalto adopted *Acceptera's* model of organic planning in order to make Finland part of 'A-Europe' in a proposition to restructure the country internally. In an article, 'The Geography of the Housing Question',[12] he shared their opinion that organic planning translated to new infrastructures – highways, railroads, telecommunication and radio – which organised people and places into an interconnected network. **(Figure 3)** As a result, old hierarchies between city and country, centre and periphery, had started to disappear leaving an organic well-functioning whole, which also facilitated the ultimate modern experience: the shrinking of time and distance through travel.

Indeed, Aalto's article might seem like mere plagiarism if it weren't for the photographs that accompanied it. If those used in *Acceptera* merely catalogued and illustrated the differences between A- and B-Europe by depicting farmers with modern machinery contrasted with horses pulling ploughs, etc, Aalto's demonstrated Moholy's influence. He used the techniques employed by Moholy – close-ups, oblique shots, and aerial views – to turn landscape, settlements and infrastructure into graphic forms that appeared as the instant imprint of

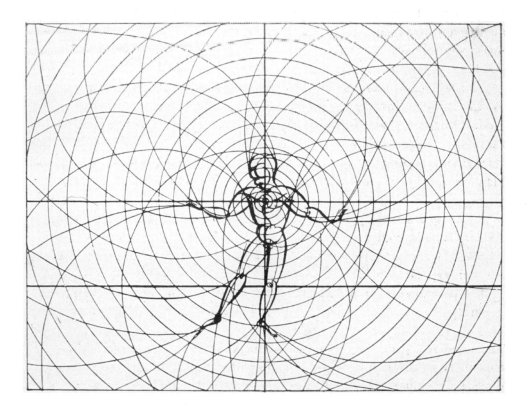

3.
Oskar Schlemmer,
'A Dancing Figure',
from *Bühne in Bauhaus*, edited by
Laszlo Moholy-Nagy,
1924

Eeva Pelkonen

the dynamic processes of modernisation. The choice of aerial views staked a claim for the expansiveness of the modern understanding of time and space. **(Figure 4)** In *From Materials to Architecture,* Moholy has this to say about photography: 'Through photography we can participate in new experiences of space . . . With [the photographers'] help, and that of the new school of architects, we have an enlargement and sublimation of our appreciation of space, the comprehension of a new spatial culture.'[13]

Moholy believed that photography not only reproduced reality but could be used to discover reality and to enhance man's understanding of the processes of modernisation, particularly the new concept of space and time.[14] Aalto's chosen illustrations demonstrate what he learnt from Moholy: that different forces – both natural and man-made – were visually manifest everywhere around us. They also suggested that the scale of technological transformation in the environment made old distinctions between man-made and natural obsolete. Indeed, Aalto did not distinguish between nature and technology. Both realms were visually manifested on the surface of the earth. Aalto called this 'land urbanisation', a combination of landform, habitations and modern infrastructure all following the organisational principle of nature:

> The telephone, with its trunk lines, local exchanges, and branch lines, is organisationally the closest thing possible to *the biological order of nature, the communication between locally clustered cells . . .* The economy of the telephone, however, leads to an organic ramification of housing areas, *permitting geographical decentralisation, but calling for local clusters.*[15]

The notion of land urbanisation made sense for Finland, whose population and industry were dispersed and far apart. Seventy per cent of the country's population still lived in rural areas, most of them on small farms. Also, the facilities for producing paper and lumber were distributed in small local towns along the main water routes. Aalto proposed new ways of settling the countryside, which would bridge the gap between country and city by producing a series of smaller semiurban areas in the form of cluster settlements, organised around major infrastructures both natural and man-made (rivers, highways, railways). This model also allowed the distribution of institutions (schools, hospitals) to serve the dispersed population. At times Aalto's model reads as a critique of centralised urbanisation and the very cities he had come to love – Stockholm, Paris and Berlin:

> Industrialism has given rise in its infancy to an uncritical centralisation of population; in the future, counterbalancing forces will come into play. Every new invention facilitates communication between people in some way, and distances are becoming irrelevant to them. Anything that is unsound and exaggerated in the town-country relationship will fall away naturally, and be replaced by equilibrium.[16]

ALVAR AALTO

BOSTADSFRÅGANS GEOGRAFI

Storstáden i sin reala form eller som embryot i allt vad befolkningsanhopning och produktionskoncentrering innebär är en direkt produkt av industrialismen. Dess nära nog absoluta kontrastförhållande till landet — landsorten och dess individualism — är allom bekant, ehuru få göra sig mödan att undersöka vad kontrasten i verkligheten innebär. — I korthet: vi ha två livsformer (stad och land) — A- och B-Europa ha de kallats — där ett flertal livsfunktioner ha olika praktisk lösning. Av den summariska tillväxt som kommit A till del uppstår ett för vår planlösa kultur typiskt kontrastförhållande med desorganiserande verkan för utvecklingen.

Följande påståenden ha ofta gjorts: den industriella utvecklingen, de tillämpade vetenskaperna, uppfinningar etc. innebära icke enbart koncentreringstendenser, man kan alltid hos dem finna även en motsatt tendens — uppfinningar som underlätta decentraliserade bostadsformer, organiseringsmöjligheter för trafik och samfärdsel, distansernas minskning genom snabbare fortskaffningsmedel, förbättring av personlig kontakt — trots distanser — genom telefon och radio etc.

4.
Alvar Aalto, Title page of 'Geography of the Housing Question' from *Arkitektur och Samhålle*, ed. Sven Markelius, 1932

Eeva Pelkonen

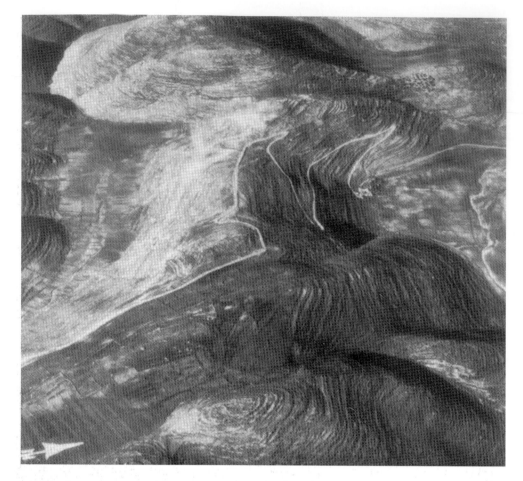

5.
Alvar Aalto, Aerial
view of agricultural
fields from
'Geography of the
Housing Question'
from *Arkitektur och
Samhålle*, ed. Sven
Markelius, 1932

Aalto's sudden attention to the countryside echoed the curious convergence of nationalism and internationalism, urban and rural culture, which came to characterise Finnish debates around Modernism. Indeed, Erkki Vala, of the literary group Torch Bearers, presented very similar ideas about decentralisation in 1929:

> UNTIL NOW Helsinki was considered the nerve centre of Finnish intellectual life.

> WE CLAIM that the country's intellectual life does not have any single nerve centre. It has multiple nervecentres.

> UNTIL NOW only the intellectual life of the capital has triggered interest.

> WE ARE GOING TO follow also the intellectual movements of the countryside.[17]

The emphasis on decentralisation and restructuring of the countryside continued to gain urgency in the early 1930s when the economic downturn led to the emergence of the extreme right; and it remains an urgent issue today.

6.
Laszlo Moholy-Nagy,
'Megastructure
Copperplate', from
*From Material to
Architecture*, 1927

Notes

1. Other participants in the exhibition included Erik Bryggman who designed a living room for the show and PE Blomstedt who designed a hotel room.
2. Alvar Aalto, 'Our Apartments as Problems' in Christian Schild (ed) *Alvar Aalto in His Own Words*, Rizzoli (New York), 1998, p 78.
3. Ibid.
4. Raoul France defined the concept in *Die Pflanze als Erfinder* (1920), which was widely read and debated among Bauhaus teachers and students in the 1920s as well as among the *Circle* group of artists and critics, which included Ben Nicholson, Naum Gabo and the art critic Philip Morton Shand.

Eeva Pelkonen

5. See Laszlo Moholy's photo-essay 'Dynamik der Gross-stadt' (Dynamism of the metropolis) in *Malerei, Fotografie, Film*, Albert Langen Verlag (Munich), 1922, pp 120–2.

6. Aalto, op cit, p 78.

7. Aalto had probably acquired a copy of *From Marterials to Architecture* during his visit to the Frankfurt CIAM conference in 1929.

8. Oskar Schlemmer," Mensch und Kunstfigur" in *Bühne im Bauhaus*, ed. Laszlo Moholy-Nagy, Albert Langen Verlag (Munich), 1924, p 15. Author's translation.

9. Aalto, op cit, p 77.

10. Gunnar Asplund, Wolter Gahn, Sven Markelius, Gregor Paulsson, Eskil Sundahl, Uno Åhren, *Acceptera*, Tidens Förlag (Stockholm), 1931, p 16. Author's translation.

11. The issue was edited by Sven Markelius and included texts by Aalto and the editor, as well as by Gregor Paulsson, Sven Wallander, Gunnar Myrdal, Markelius, Roul Henningsen, Gotthard Johansson, Stig Odeen and Viking Göransson.

12. Aalto, 'The Geography of a Housing Question' in Christian Schild (ed), *Alvar Aalto in His Own Words*, Rizzoli (New York), 1998, p 87.

13. Laszlo Moholy-Nagy, *Von Material zu Architektur*, Passavia Druckerei (Passau), 1929, p 111.

14. My discussion of Moholy-Nagy's photographs has been informed by Eleanor M Hight, *Picturing Modernism: Moholy-Nagy and photography in Weimar*, MIT Press (Cambridge, Mass),1995.

15. Aalto, 'The Geography of a Housing Question', p 87.

16. Christian Schild (ed), *Alvar Aalto in His Own Words,* Rizzoli (New York), 1998, p 187. Author's translation.

17. Erkki Vala, 'Uusi vuosi – uusi aika', *Tulenkantajat*, 1/192 (1929), p 11.

4

Ahmet Omurtag

What is an Organism?

According to one common-sense view organisms are entities that struggle. They struggle to live, to survive, to exist. They battle against one another, as prey against predator; they compete for food, for sources of energy and for space to live in. If there had been sufficient resources for all, one can imagine that the basis and reason for competition would not have existed. Hence, underlying the reality of organisms as struggling entities is a basic condition of scarcity.

In addition to the battle against one another, there is another sense of the notion of struggle. This is the struggle that organisms carry out against, so to speak, indifference – the indifference associated simply with the fact that inanimate matter has no recognition of the concerns and purposes of organisms. The kind of organisations associated with living things do not spontaneously appear out of the random shuffling of materials. This idea has been made more precise, even quantitatively precise, as I will briefly explain below. It implies that not only are there not enough resources to go around; but, in addition, whatever does exist of useful and good things has a tendency to disintegrate and be dissipated. Organisms also face the scarcity of time. This introduces an element of unrest and transforms scarcity into a fundamental mode of existence for them.

The world poses for the organism a fatal threat, not because of its maliciousness but because inanimate materials simply have no intentions at all. As such, they are alien to entities that are organised in special ways and strive to realise certain goals. One could say, for this reason, that organisms live in a 'disenchanted' environment. This brings into view the idea of a mental struggle, against the impending disintegration of all significance and meaning.

Living bodies were not always seen in this light. I would like to invoke an image of nature, prevalent during the Renaissance according to historians, which considers living things as part of a network of significant analogies and systems of meaningful resemblances. Today it is hard to imagine the scale and weight of a world-view like this – especially with so little time. Nevertheless let me attempt this by quoting a historian of ideas, Michel Foucault: in times of old, men of knowledge believed that the task of knowledge 'was to uncover a language that God had previously distributed across the face of the earth.'[1] The signs thus scattered in the world established semantic relationships, and knowledge had to rely on finding these signs. They were there precisely so that they could be found. This presents an environment that was far from being alien to the purposive activities, cares, delights and worries of organisms, especially human beings.

A radical distinction between organic and inorganic beings did not arise within this framework. In its stead was repeated Aristotle's idea of a continuous hierarchy of nature, *Scala Naturae*, in which one could pass with small changes from minerals to plants, and all the way to human beings, and even perhaps to God.

I mention this merely as a contrast to the modern view of organisms that has become dominant in science since the early 19th century. Passing over centuries I come directly to the three basic ideas already then prevalent:

1. Organisms contain no special substances or insubstantial properties that endow them with unique characteristics. They are constructed of the same basic elements of which things inorganic are built.
2. The parts of organisms are assembled and function together in order to achieve purposes: they are made of ordinary materials organised in extraordinary ways.
3. They actively maintain this organisation through exchange with their environment.

These ideas go together with an emphasis on the binary distinction between organic and inorganic entities, as opposed to the several 'kingdoms' of naturalists. This new distinction was also opposed to more recent mechanistic ideas, exemplified in the work of Descartes, which saw no need for it since all of nature was a machine.

A famous physiologist of the late 18th century, George Cuvier, made the following very modern observation about organisms: Around the living being there is a continual circulation from the outside to the inside and from the inside to the outside, constantly maintained and yet fixed within certain limits. Thus, living bodies should be considered as kinds of furnaces into which dead substances are successively introduced in order to combine together in various ways. He says elsewhere that 'dead substances are borne toward living bodies in order to take up a place and exert an action . . . in order to escape from them again one day so as to fall once more under the laws of inanimate nature.'[2]

One could perhaps draw a line of conceptual descent from this to current physical ideas, such as 'dissipative structures', developed by physicists and chemists trying to understand complex behaviour.

Biology today knows a great amount of detail about how organisms accomplish their goals. We know the molecular mechanisms that attack foodstuffs in the cell and break them down into energy-bearing and other useful structures, how these are distributed, how various functions are regulated, how their waste is collected and disposed. Since the 1950s there has also been a mathematical theory of nerve signalling and a basic understanding of the mechanisms of heredity. One of the most striking findings of this theory is that all known functions are accomplished by similar kinds of molecular machinery throughout the world of organisms, from bacteria to human beings. We may all be the descendants of a cell that existed in a puddle at the beginning of the Cambrian period about 600 million years ago. This cell had solved its problems in some specific way, by no means the only possible one, and the biosphere has inherited its machinery. None of this wealth of information contradicts the framework established by early modern physiology and summarised by the analogy of an organism as a 'furnace' in Cuvier's observation.

Since Darwin, we are also coming to realise how entities that can have goals and intentions could arise and undergo changes over geological periods of time. According to the theory of evolution, organisms that exist at any period are the products of a unique history saturated with contingencies which have been integrated into their bodies. The past is an intrinsic part of their current structure. Life, consequently, is an irreducible mixture of contingencies and physical mechanisms.

Although based on chance mutations, the long-term dynamics of evolution and the formation and modification of species proceed with a necessity of their own. Evolution by natural selection, Darwin said, 'depends on what we call spontaneous or accidental variability. Let an architect be compelled to build an edifice with uncut stones, fallen from a precipice. The shape of each fragment may be called accidental'.[3] This is because although 'the shape of each has been determined by natural laws . . . there is no relation between these laws and the purpose for which each fragment is used by the builder'. Similarly, Darwin continues, 'the variations of each creature are determined by fixed and immutable laws; but these bear no relation to the living structure which is slowly built up through the power of selection.'[4]

The material making up the organism is arranged in a highly specific manner. If we imagine all the different ways in which the same materials could have been arranged, the actual organisation found in the organisms appears as a tiny subset of the full set of physical possibilities. The configurations contained in this subset have, therefore, a very small probability of emerging spontaneously as a result of random shuffling. This contains an important underlying idea: the distribution of probability over the space of possible arrangements must be uniform. That is, random shuffling will cause a system to visit each configuration equally often. A hurricane blowing through a junkyard does not assemble

Ahmet Omurtag

together a Boeing 747, to use the vivid imagery of Fred Hoyle, because that is a very special arrangement – like the organism. The improbability of the structures related to an organism is understood in a similar sense. Organisms are constantly trying, at all levels, to sort and order what nature tends to shuffle and dissipate.

I mentioned above that nature's indifference can be cast in quantitative form. This has been achieved by the science of statistical thermodynamics. Whether through Boltzmann's 'Stosszahlansatz', the 'ergodic hypothesis' or the assumption of 'equal a priori probabilities', one is led by the admirably successful and accurate theory of statistical thermodynamics to the idea, in mathematical form, that inanimate nature is indifferent to the complex arrangements that organisms need in order to live. An important and well-known consequence of this theory, the Second Law of Thermodynamics, makes a related assertion: improbable complex arrangements correspond to states of low entropy and in an isolated system starting with low entropy, the entropy must inevitably increase in time. This can be translated into the impending death of an isolated organism and forms part of an organism's essence. Thermodynamics, amid industrial engines and gushes of steam, not only discovered the omnipresence of time, but has also shaped our view of organisms as beings that struggle.

Notes

1. Michel Foucault, *The Order of Things*, Vintage Books (New York), 1970, p 242.
2. Georges Cuvier, quoted in S. Shapin, *The Scientific Revolution*, University of Chicago Press, 1998, p 76.
3. Charles Darwin, *The Origin of the Species*, Bantam (New York), 1999, p 40.
4. Ibid.

5

Panellists: Ruth Berthold, Deborah Gans, Zehra Kuz,
Ahmet Omurtag, Eeva Pelkonen

Panel Discussion

Deborah Gans: The title of this session, Evolution, refers both to a historical line of descent of the organic from German Romanticism through Häring and Scharoun and to the idea of *formfinden*, or form finding, presented by Ahmet in a biological and Zehra in an architectural sense. I'd like to begin by asking Eeva to address Aalto's relation to this Germanic tradition and to the mode of the organic.

Eeva Pelkonen: Aalto had close contact with the German architectural scene from 1929 onwards when he attended the CIAM (Congrès International de l'Architecture Moderne) in Frankfurt. He met Hugo Häring at the meeting, but developed closer contact with Laszlo Moholy-Nagy, whose notion of 'biotechnique' he engaged in his writings and architectural work. 'Biotechnique' differed from Häring's idea of organic form in putting more emphasis on how man occupied and experienced space as dynamic, expansive and interconnected. Modern technology and infrastructure – railroads, highways, telephones – played a significant role in facilitating this experience. One must remember that Häring's approach to form and function had by that time come under attack by Le Corbusier and Theo van Doesburg who condemned it as 'dogmatic functionalism'. Aalto, eager to become an 'international' architect, was savvy enough to keep away from Häring, whose position was rather peripheral within the international Modern Movement.

It is true that Aalto and the Germans share a major history and appear as a major unity of northern European organicism; however, I would argue that

there is a fundamental difference between them that linked Aalto to other Scandinavian figures. Häring first of all has a fully fledged theory and design method of organicism, as opposed to Aalto, who makes you read between the lines. In this theory Häring emphasises the notion of inner unity, of form arising from the inner essence of the building, in most cases from the function. The organicism grows from inside out, a romantic notion. Whereas Aalto, when he is talking about organicism, doesn't emphasise the inner organisation of form in isolation, except as the idea of the psychological function of architecture. For Aalto, organic architecture has much more to do with the network of relationships than with the notion of the organic unity of a building or a city. I don't think Häring necessarily implied that the medieval was the *one* organic community; but he did view it as *Gemeinschaft* (as opposed to modern *Gesellschaft*) with an inner unity, an inner essence within the boundaries of that community. When Aalto talks about the organic society, he first of all talks about the modern society. He thinks modern society is far more organic than former agricultural societies because it has more relationships and infrastructures that allow people to communicate with one another.

Gans: Does the psychological dimension open up the strictly dialectical relationships between individual/collective public/private (and subject/object) often found in Modernism – as in Le Corbusier's 'inseparable binomial of the individual and collectivity'? For example, does Aalto think of a public building for the community in terms of a collective psychology or does he imagine that it can address individual perception in its more idiosyncratic and least typological aspects. Or, in the end, do he and Häring sustain the split.

Zehra Kuz: I want to ask Eeva to clarify the discussion of community versus society. Many German social scientists brought up similar arguments at the turn of the century when they were rewriting utopia, democracy and the German dream. As a matter of fact it was in Germany that the intensity of industrialisation escalated, if not doubled, during that time and the theoretical output on social sciences was unparalleled. Toennies' and Endell's theories on *Gemeinschaft* and *Gesellschaft* are based on methods of organisation and relationships, rather than just the agrarian activity. Community should not be described exclusively with the term 'agricultural'. Weber's *Die Stadt* analyses the city as a political concept for economic profit, in other words as the political commerce which, according to these theories, disrupts the organic wholeness of the city. Sombart distinguishes between cities of consumption and cities of production, etc. In all the subsequent writings of contemporary German social scientists, the focus was on the system, how it had to be organised; the scale remains very ambivalent. Although it was not known at the time whether or not it would be the answer to the dilemma, the Werkbund was formed to soothe the conflicts of these social forces. The metropolis was an accepted reality. I think that the nature of system was critical, not the scale.

I don't think Häring intended to design for the individual. Haring's work should be viewed in its concurrent place, time and culture. However, Scharoun's architectural work can be seen as an extension of Häring's theories. Their approach, in theory and practice, was designing the space around the event; fusing the user with the space intrinsically, such as in the Berlin Philharmonic building and its concert hall. This approach is evident in Aalto's work as well as Scharoun's and, of course, in Häring's writings. Can you elaborate more about Aalto's sense of the relationship of community and society?

Pelkonen: The question of how to mediate between different scales was central to the debates. Organicism always implied an idea of structural organisation where different elements are brought together into a well-functioning whole. Homes form cities, which are part of regions, etc. Implied in this model was a social argument – individuals form families, which form societies, etc. Organicism was a means to mediate these relationships and bring about a society which, like nature, would never go out of balance. This organic approach also had a Pan-European constituency. In fact, *Acceptera*, published by the Swedish group of architects involved in the Stockholm Exhibition of the 1930s, approached organicism from this point of view. For them, organic, that is modern, industrial societies, differed from agrarian societies by being interconnected and interdependent on one another. It is telling that this organicism gained popularity after the First World War when this balance had been lost.

I would further emphasise the technological aspect of the debate. In Germany in the 1920s, following the introduction of Taylorism and Fordism and other forms of production, cultural modernisation simultaneously created a backlash. Häring was part of the reaction while Aalto embraced modernisation as bringing advantages including technology. He was part of the group of Swedish architects in the 1930s who thought modern technology could mediate between individual and society, kind of like Frank Lloyd Wright in his love of the telephone as an individual mouthpiece through which you can communicate with the whole world. With the telephone, you can be separate from the

community, participate in the society, but still be more individual. The infrastructure creates this totally ideal condition where individuality and society embrace one another.

Gans: Is this globalism or a culturally specific condition?

Pelkonen: Aalto wanted to have it both ways. The model was concentric in the sense that a smaller unit or individual was always conceived as being part of

some larger whole. So understood, organic architecture could be national and international, individual and societal at the same time. It is also telling that Aalto started to talk about organic architecture when he was constantly travelling.

Gans: Also, you can be urban and rural at the same time. We heard it last night from Behnisch. As I understand him, Behnisch's desire for the continuity of interior and exterior is also a desire for the continuity of urban and rural, and of community and property. The Munich Olympic Stadium with which he has become symbolically linked is such a landscape without walls. And, as he commented with charm last night, he thinks its roof is too strong. In this regard, Ahmet's talk is humbling because he is telling us that beneath the idyll of the Munich park is a disenchanted environment. Ahmet, is there a biological equivalent of an enchanted landscape or utopian pastorale of the sort depicted by Behnisch and Aalto? And to follow up, is there freedom for lower organisms in some regard to their behaviour?

Ahmet Omurtag: Briefly my answer to both questions would be yes. In a scientific framework, can one think about an enchanted environment? Yes, because, although scientifically speaking there is no escaping the fact that an organism or a specially organised structure has to run into a disenchanted wall at some point, the boundaries can be pushed far enough away from the individual organism for it to actually experience something like what we call enchantment. This would be a description of an ecosystem. In other words, all organisms have an internal rhythm which has a certain constancy and stability.

well as the Berlin Philharmonic. In the concert hall every seat is a good seat. It is a gathering place, a collective space and it has excellent acoustical qualities.

William Katavolos (audience): Can Eeva comment on Aalto's notion of how form grew by itself, so that Ahmet can comment upon it? Aalto spoke of the municipality; but he also described how the house began as a single cell and each room divided and subdivided. His analogy was incredibly biological. I remember this statement from 30 years ago when he made it. Can you put Aalto in biological terms right now?

Pelkonen: This is a sequel to Zehra's comment really. All organic architecture in its notion of purpose implies, somehow, a dehumanised architecture in the power of function to create form. The organic function takes the maker out to a certain extent. It's always implied in organicism that, besides the individual creator's will, there is some power elsewhere that is able to create architecture. Of course, the celebration of vernacular architecture can be interpreted similarly in that it has a creator who is innocent of architectural language.

Gans: The vernacular as a set of inherited traits rather than an individually authored event.

Pelkonen: Yes.

Omurtag: It's not really responding to the question, but the actual process of biological evolution by natural selection also has no creator and still leads to the generation of very complicated organisms. I don't know the architect you speak of, but this may pose for you a useful analogy. Very complicated and purposeful organisms can be built out of such processes. Sometimes these selections work much, much better than designing programs, as engineers are beginning to realise nowadays. Programmers are now using what they call genetic algorithms which introduce random mutations to a given computer code. If it works they keep it. If it doesn't work, they try another. This way, they evolve codes that work much, much better than those deliberately designed by programmers.

8.
House on Mount Desert Island, Maine, 1992, Northwest Elevation, Gans & Jelacic Architects

emphasis on the internal structure that persists within chance encounters. Similarly, Behnisch didn't seem that interested in tectonics as an ordering device, or function as a determinant of organisation. The thing that is free is free from programme and from structural restraint. So I am asking, within your discussion of the responsiveness of the plan, what is the persistent structure? And alternatively, how random can the architecture be?

Kuz: I would like to step back; the discipline of architecture as a profession is very structural and systematic, and building activity is sequential. Randomness in architecture is an open-ended question. However, ideas evolve. What begins as 'responsiveness' can be transformed and developed. The house plans of Häring have an 'ideal flow diagram', which evolves around daily life. Rooms aren't quite randomly placed. Their location is in response to the sun, for example: the study faces west; the bedrooms face east; the living room exploits the best view; entrances are from the north. There is a certain grammar or prevailing strategy but the geometry seems arbitrary; it makes room for randomness to take place. I believe that Häring used 'purposefulness' as an excuse to explore his ideas on the new aesthetic and test his theory. The house is a personable and familiar scenario for everyone. Also, these are simply the seeds of the organic found in historical references. I don't want to be locked into the history during this discussion. Events evolve, cultures too.

Pelkonen: Here I should remind us that it is difficult to talk about some constant reading of organicism in Aalto's work, apart from its implication of a morally superior approach to design. Increasingly from about 1930 on Aalto used organic analogy to refer to a certain type of design process, where forms grow as if naturally unmediated by reason. Aalto's material studies of laminated wood represented this approach. He talked about the freedom of form to evolve without constraints like function or preconceived architectural language. Yet this freedom and openess was at the same time based on a very specific technique. I would agree with Zehra that organic strategy, independent of its formal outcome, is based on obsession with the particular.

Regarding the purposiveness of randomness, Aalto's idea of organicism is close to Ahmet's. First you let form evolve; then it makes as-if-random encounters with function through which it becomes more functional than a form thought of as functional. The alternating forms he uses repeatedly at various scales and for various purposes – vases, suspended ceilings, door handles – stay the same but without an intended single function. They gain different functional readings through random encounters, if you wish, as in your marketplace.

Omurtag: This comment reminds me that for many organisms there are also selecting agents. Otherwise, no structure would be built. The important questions are: firstly, what is the selecting agent doing and, secondly, how big are the chunks it is selecting for? If random things are happening, and you wait to select until it is an entire cathedral, you will wait a long time. Eventually the

11.
Private Residence,
Austria, 2000,
Detail of Porch,
Zehra Kuz, architect

cathedral will appear, but you will have a centrally designed entity. Whereas, if you have an agent selecting just a column or window, then something else will appear in the end. The selecting agent is very important. You can't assume it is left out of the process of organic building of a structure, of any structure.

Matthew Jelacic (audience): I have a question for Ahmet that refers back to Eeva's distinction between *Gemeinschaft* and *Gesellschaft*. Behnisch in his lecture seemed resistant to large housing projects and more sympathetic to the small, community models. Can we extrapolate your model, Ahmet, to suggest a comfortable organicism for the city that is more complex than either the agrarian *Gemeinschaft* or Behnisch's preference? From a biological standpoint, what happens at large scales and in complex environments? Could you suggest a model for a more densely inhabited setting that could still be organic in the terms of Behnisch's work?

Omurtag: I understand your question to ask if we can have an individual living comfortably in a large structured environment. Organic integration of a larger

14.
Dienstleistungs-
gebäude der
Landesgirokasse,
Stuttgart, 1997,
Behnisch, Sabatke,
Behnisch and
Partners, architects

that a theatre is used for a gymnasium and vice versa. Due to the flexibility, their respective functions may be impaired. But, then again, organisms are specific to surroundings. There are airborne organisms, waterborne organisms.

Rossant: But they have a life. Buildings don't.

Gans: Maybe Aldo Rossi proposed an organic city in such a way that type and flexibility aren't contradictory. He didn't see the organic as exclusive of type. As a skeletal structure that 'grows' through accretion, his city depends on the persistence of type. When I look at the plans of Scharoun, Aalto and Behnisch, I see a similar sensibility where, within the outline of the architecture, are set pieces that are recognisable by figure. They telegraph somehow their typological history — as amphitheatre or auditorium or library. The approach is one of layering. Rather than setting a hierarchy and absorbing everything within it, this architecture allows fragments of typological figures to persist within the a-perspectival space – or whatever organisation they've got. I don't mind using Rossi as an example here because it suggests some odd connections between the Modernist organic and other occurrences. John Johansen, in his writings, is similarly inclusive of this Post-Modern sensibility within his commitment to the organic.

John Johansen (audience): There are types, prototypes, archetypes and parts of building types – like stairs. These building types were established and sustained by people and the society who built them. There are also prototypes in nature, of course. A tree is a tree not because of DNA but because of the thing they call memory. It's a prototype. A tree remembers what trees have been for the millions of years before them; and this is how nature transfers prototypes.

Buscescu: John, yes, I believe this issue of type relates to memory but the tree isn't a sufficiently precise example. Shelbridge talks of 'morphic resonance'. He treats types and patterns of memories in nature not as universal law but as habits. He takes it out of the scientific model or introduces an artificial model for nature in which nature develops habits. They aren't infinite in time or space; they are local. It may be that type is a form of memory. Morphic resonance for Shelbridge is a religious model, in the end, because we carry it within ourselves. I don't particularly like that.

Gans: I can't resist pointing out the importance of memory to Rossi as well. Memory is a conflation of the individual experience and collective history – if not exactly the organic bridge between the two that we find in Ruskin.

Pelkonen: Here we should revisit the famous Werkbund debate of 1914, which posed Hermann Muthesius against Henry van de Velde on the issue of typification and individual creativity. Aalto also criticised standardisation and typification from the organicist perspective. Instead of the production of sameness based on the logic of the machine, he called for variability, based on how a single cell in nature can adapt to different conditions and functional tasks. In the same way, he talked about adapting to complex psychological needs. A presumably creative open-ended process rather than a mechanised one was thought of as the better means to understand the complexity of human life, which had come to be understood as a dynamic entity. It is not coincidental that Aalto starts using metaphorical allusions to nature at the same time in the late 1930s.

Katavolos: At that time – 1914 – the choice was simple: the *typisierung* (type production) or the *kunstswollen* (will to form). Could you explain Muthesius and the *kuntswollen* group in relation to these terms – why one group went one way, one the other? The things you talk about are still real and important for our students to understand: the artist's will or the type. Muthesius ran side by side with van de Velde and that parallelism continued until the First World War. How are the terms unique? What makes them different from the terms we use today?

Kuz: This is related to industrialisation, especially mode of production. The question at hand wasn't only the aesthetics of the form, but how to optimise production. This initiated the split between the so-called organicists and other Modernists, who created Werkbund and later the Bauhaus. One group was interested in developing the 'typus' the other the *gestalt*.

Muthesius and van de Velde ran side by side as long as they were advocating change. The definition of 'change' was, however, a complicated matter. Muthesius voted for standardisation and van de Velde for creative freedom. Theodor Fischer, who was a founding member, left the Werkbund for the same reason as van de Velde. It was a crucial moment in history when the Modernists' agenda split into different paths or, can one say, approaches.

Katavolos: For Behnisch, the issue is the same. Is this mass production or one of a kind?

Kuz: He is very clear on this aspect. Apparently, he did not pursue methods of mass production after the early days; it wasn't what he wanted to explore. In Behnisch's buildings every single element contributes to the overall expression of the project, in a one-of-a-kind way. Also the design practice in Günter Behnisch's office is, from what we were told yesterday, refreshingly undetermined and democratic. The design process or methods are not engraved or repeated unless a veteran's memory is at work.

Jelacic: I think it's now possible to collapse the difference between type and uniqueness in mass production because of the computer programs available. When Gaetano Pesce spoke at Pratt in 1996, he described his use of CADCAM software to create unique forms within mass production. Every piece is unique but it is based on a type of mass production.

Pelkonen: It is called customised mass production.

Tom Brigham: An example of that would be cabbage patch baby dolls.

Rossant: I believe that there are now bionic structures with instances of highly individualised function within form that is somewhat constant.

Omurtag: The question of types is a most beautiful thing in evolutionary biology. Natural selection always has to make use of the existing structures to solve new problems. It is always tinkering. That is why organisms get more and more complicated. It never starts from ground zero.

Part II

Transformations

Morph: Kitchen Utensils to Man and Ape

Photo credit: Tom Brigham

6

Volker Giencke

Work

My interest in the organic approach began in the late 1960s and early 1970s when I worked with Merete Mattern, a German architect and the daughter of Herman Mattern and Hedda Anbacher, the landscape architects who worked with Hans Scharoun. So, in the early years when I was particularly studying the ideas of Scharoun and the idea of a building as an organic wholeness, they made me aware of how architecture becomes part of the landscape.

One of the problems of organic architecture is that it can only be defined by architectural example and social history; and yet, if the architecture of our time is to have any public and social significance, it has to solve problems specific to our time. The notion of organic architecture is expressed through its shape, the structure of which is just as important as the form. The organic's most exciting and most important principle is precisely that it does not follow any formalistic and geometric rules and is removed from any special method. There is no theory, no manual to follow. Organic architecture happens beyond rectangular geometric shapes. Also, it has no obligation to follow free forms or to create something deconstructive or plastic. It follows or combines all styles and fashions to become inexplicable.

Organic architecture shows that there are other criteria besides function and construction. Just like art, architecture doesn't depend on outside influence but presents itself as an organic subject, following organic actions. For me, the organic happens when the architect starts to play, not as a challenge, not as superficial play, but as a playfulness through which the subject of architecture is expressed beyond the obstacles of function, construction, form and material.

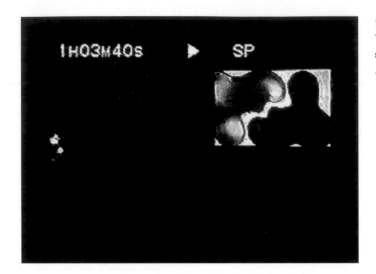

1.
Volker Giencke lecturing with slide of glass vases of Alvar Aalto 1936

The mastery of form, function and construction of form become the prerequisites for the built architecture but not the architecture as a discipline. The architect is like a chef, who doesn't depend on the ingredients and raw material, which he uses, but rather on the special mixture, which he accomplishes. Also, the master chef's creation is not dictated by the tastes of the guests. The same thing goes for architecture. It is a master's creation. It can't be taught or explained. It becomes (by example) self-evident. In this regard, Hugo Häring was the father of organic architecture, but less of an organic architect than Hans Scharoun and Alvar Aalto, who were less so than Frei Otto and Frank Gehry. Let me now take you through a brief personal history of organic thought.

Hans Scharoun was one of the few German architects with an international reputation who stayed in Germany during the Second World War. I am fascinated by his efforts to resist the restrictions which the German government imposed on modern architecture at that time. During the mid-1930s he built a single-family home in Berlin. As seen from the street side, the house looks nothing but regional. Scharoun was very clever – he copied the tilt of the roof from Hitler's own Bavarian house. The garden side is different; the path takes one through different levels. The roof follows the free form of the terraces. It is a small but fine example of an organic architecture. Later, when he was prevented from building anything for a period of time, he started drawing and painting visionary architecture and architecture for exhibitions. During the 1950s and 1960s he became the most famous German architect.

For Alvar Aalto, who did not speak much and started his work with a bottle of Italian wine, the approach to architecture was different. As an architect, he was extremely aware of social responsibilities. He did not restrict himself to architecture. He mostly addressed the design of interiors according to materials. His famous glass vases of 1936 exhibit the real potential of the material and that of the corresponding forms. Therefore these vases are much more architectural than any contemporary building. (**Figure 1**) Likewise, the Paimio chair of 1930 is a very dynamic chair. It is still influencing my approach to architecture 60 years later. It is not mere furniture; it is not architecture. It is a piece of art.

And then there is Le Corbusier, who approached the organic as he drew the human hand and yet was the most progressive architect of his time. The Villa Savoie showed his strength in its glass wall, which was the biggest glass panel wall of the time. The wall could be removed so that one could open the living space of the house to the terraces. He tried to erase the borderline that exists between the outside and the inside. He tried to overcome boundaries.

Frei Otto is the German 'konstructeure'. In German this means the person who is able to combine construction and architecture, which allows me to call him the Leonardo of the century. The Voliere, the house of birds, in Munich is a lesser-known project of his. It is an architecture with a skin of wire mesh, a very fine wire mesh. It is an architecture that disappears – which is one of the many wonderful qualities of organic architecture.

In 1980 the first architecture biennale in Venice, The Presence of the Past, included 'La Strada Novissima' exhibition at Corderie dell'Arsenale and a first opportunity to see Frank Gehry's architecture. The task was to design an exhibition area, between the columns and behind the facades. Gehry built an entrance to the space that looked as if he had run out of money. I liked it. It was refreshing. For me it was refreshing and therefore also organic. Gehry's single-family house from 18 years ago, for the artist Ron Davis in Malibu, is one of the most outstanding single homes I know. It is nothing but a simple concept. It is an empty space that has different heights because it is built over distorted squares, and stairs which connect them. There are spaces with stairs which, like furniture, create a material landscape, a wonderful artificial topography.

Finally, I would like to present Oscar Niemeyer as an organic thinker. In his headquarters for the French Communist Party in Paris, a project of the 1960s, the façade of the office building in the background is a response to the government, but the entrance to the building leads one storey down from the ground-floor platform to where the main assembly hall is located, and that hall looks surreal. Oscar Niemeyer's last project, a museum in Brazil finished when he was 90 years old, looks like a flying saucer. This building exhibits his confidence and his emotions about his work, about architecture. It exhibits his playfulness, in that there were difficulties in constructing and engineering his design.

While I was working for Merete Mattern during the late 1960s and early 1970s I designed two family homes under her supervision. **(Figure 2)** These are buildings with great emotional content. They also show the greatest technical achievement I was capable of at that time. The project is an example of the influence of science and philosophy. At that time, Merete had strong connections with philosophers and scientists, and I call this complex of hers 'organic' because of the influence of the philosophers. I am thinking of Octavio Paz's *The Thought and Everything Else*. In it, he proclaims the thought to be the only way of common living that does not disrespect the human being. Thought, stability . . . On the other hand, thought creates the criteria such as special longing, curiosity and surprise. Both are aspects of organic being.

When we began the conceptual work on the botanical gardens in Graz in 1982, the glass house as an expression for the modern in architecture no longer

Volker Giencke

2.
**Site Model by Merete
Mattern**

existed. The cast-iron and steel construction of the 19th-century greenhouses in the capital of the Austrian monarchy literally did not survive. The same should not happen to other greenhouses and botanical gardens. Also, the original idea of the greenhouse had been to create a natural environment for plants and that it should function as a space between the outside and the inside. But building a greenhouse in the 1980s was considered to be only a question of how to organise the installation of heat, ventilation and humidity control. **(Figures 3 and 4)**

Because of our desire to build an everlasting greenhouse, we decided to use aluminium. Using the aluminium turned out to be very difficult. To make it more rigid, we decided to make it parabolic and constructed from many smaller pieces. We couldn't find any mechanical/environmental engineers in Austria, so we tried to do the calculations ourselves. The design process came to a halt. At that time the design was very progressive and required a very high technical standard. Ten years after we had started the construction of the botanical greenhouse, glass technology had developed and reached a new level. We had really wanted to guarantee a higher version of transparency. We wanted to achieve a transparency with all its physical characteristics, which would allow the building to transform according to different conditions. **(Figure 5)**

In the end, the technological systems were like this:

The primary construction of the building consists of tubes which are heating pipes for running water as well as being structural. In other words, there is water running through the primary structure. So there is the primary construction of the tubes with heated water inside and the secondary structure running

3.
Botanical Gardens,
Graz, Austria, 1989:
Aerial View

4.
Botanical
Greenhouse, Graz,
Austria, 1989: Second
Floor Plan. The
botanical houses of
1850 square meters
are divided into 4
buildings for different
climates: tropical,
mediterranean,
temperate and desert,
arranged around a
broad raised square.
A pool, exterior
planting, and a
further prismatic
building covered with
an inclined glass roof,
complete the scheme

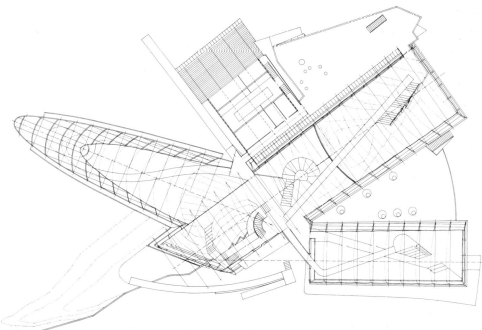

Volker Giencke

5.

Botanical Greenhouse, Graz, Austria, 1989: Exterior View. The skin wrapped around the frame is made from double pieces of un-reinforced acrylic-glass. The reduction to the minimum of the glasshouse structure has achieved an unprecedented light transmission of 98 %. The air circulation uses vents built into the floor and automatic opening flaps seen set into the tops of the arches. For the cooling, a "diffusing fog system" is employed, able to drop the temperature by 5 degrees instantly

Photo credit: Hans Georg Tropper

above. The cooling system is a new invention, which is able to cool the house instantly to about 5°C. It also creates an artificial atmosphere. The building is ventilated naturally; there are openings at the foundation level and at the top of the structure. The covers of insulated glass elements are wrapped around the structure like a skin, which is a difficult characteristic to accomplish. A very simple but clever detail of the construction of the staircase is a metal rope, which is suspended from the tube, with a soft material in between in order to protect the tube. **(Figure 6)** The construction of the greenhouse took four years, mainly because of budget problems.

The botanical gardens are near the centre of Graz, surrounded by green, and by large solitary family homes. The site is situated on a street corner in a section where no vegetation was possible before. Seen geologically, the site was a flat plane. Along the street side of the gardens is the Mediterranean house. The largest house, the Northern house, lies in the centre and the Tropical house is in the foreground of the complex. An aerial view shows the different parts as if they were scattered structures of architecture. The parabolic shapes of the

6.

Botanical Greenhouse, Graz, Austria, 1989: Detail of Frame and Suspension Detail. The joints, formed from aluminum elements, are nodes connecting the horizontal beams and distributing the watering and compressed air system. The ramps and footbridges are wooden elements suspended from these same nodal points at the top of the building

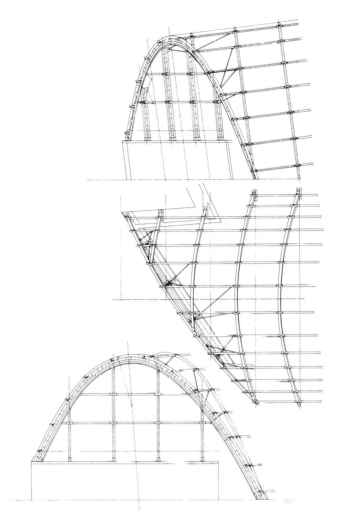

houses are different because of the height of the plants they contain. The connection between the Northern house and the Mediterranean house is a membrane, which is high tech. The transition is accomplished through this three-dimensionally suspended membrane.

As part of the interior landscape there are staircases and bridges connecting seminar rooms and exhibition areas and other facilities. Sometimes I think the plants destroyed and took over the project. On the other hand, we designed it for plants. It is a satisfying feeling. At the entrance space the staircases lead from the first-floor to the second-floor galleries. You can almost experience the plants from their roots to their tops because you move through different levels. **(Figure 7)**

Transparency is something that is an integral part of an organic architecture, as much as the mobility I have been describing is. It brings the architecture alive. Through the transparency, the expression of the greenhouse can change completely. It can be influenced by the different qualities of daylight, especially in the difference between day and night. Likewise, your experiences of the building vary. During the day, you recognise the forms of the construction of the building. At night, the opposite is true; you see the human activities inside.

Volker Giencke

During daylight the glass can be very transparent. Or, when the sun shines at a specific angle on to the building, it can appear to be a temporary skin over a landscape. When the sky is overcast the house becomes like an object, or a designed instrument. Sometimes it looks like a submarine. **(Figure 8)** During the night, if the house is illuminated from the inside, its transparency changes it completely. The structure becomes visible and you cannot see or experience the skin. A detail of the partition wall shows a very high tech membrane, a very transparent membrane . . . And here, the skin disappears.

For a new version of the rhododendron greenhouse in Bremen, northern Germany, we designed an artificial hilly landscape. The outline is defined by a membrane. **(Figure 9)** The most interesting part of the scheme is the skin, which is the reason why this project won. I had the same concept 20 years ago

**7.
Botanical
Greenhouse,
Graz, Austria, 1989:
Interior View,
Desert House**

Photo credit:
Peter Eder

for the botanical greenhouse in Graz. The skin is more or less the same as the membrane we used between the Northern house and the Mediterranean house of the earlier project. Now, I decided to cover the whole thing with one skin. All the different climate zones lie inside the high tech skin with no interior structure. The form is defined by the skin, which shapes the building.

In one of my first projects, done with Günter Domenig for the Wörthersee Shipping Company, and located near a famous lake in Austria in lovely countryside, there are big sliding roof panels and wall elements over the concrete structure. **(Figure 10)** The main concept was based on mobility. The Cushicle project from the 1960s by Michael Webb, a member of Archigram and a very

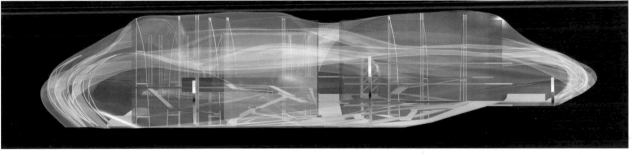

9.
Digital Rendering of Rhododendron Greenhouse, Bremen, Germany, 1997: Different climatic zones are incorporated under a single cover. A double layer, transparent ETFE foil with reinforcements welded in to resist tears is stretched over a newly created landscape. The enclosure is fireproof, self-cleaning and open to ultraviolet radiation. The plants' natural climate can thus be perfectly simulated. The internal pressure achieved by this double membrane amounts to about 500 pascals and remains stable in the open system. Warm air coming through the two-layered membrane is applied for heating and cooling using heat exchangers. The structure that bears and stretches the membrane is made of slender corrosion-resistant aluminum tubes. All installations are either directed in or clipped to these tubes

10.
Exterior View of the Wörthersee Shipping Company, Carintha 1971–81, designed with Günter Domenig.
The dockyard is conceived as an artificial island. The project proposes a sliding canopy over the dry dock,
the structural components of workshop track (red/brown), crane and railings (white/grey) having already been
placed. The roof and sliding roof-wall partitions are zinc coated

important figure in organic architecture, can be carried in a backpack and inflated when needed. It is a complete nomadic human unit – a building worn as a suit – which is self-sustained. Officially, the history of architecture starts with human settlement; but maybe this assumption is a mistake. Mobility has a physical and economic importance. I, myself, have always wanted the chance to be mobile. And then there is the desert. I dare quote Emmanuel Kant: 'Space and time do not exist as long as we do not look at them.'

In my own country, Austria, there are more mountains than desert, so there is more landscape surface. If the skin of all Austria had been stretched over a flat surface it would have been a large country. The Austrian landscape, the green fields and the hillside near Graz provided the backdrop for my house. **(Figure 11)** A white membrane in the background, which belongs to my house, and orthogonal steel construction are in contrast to the natural surroundings. **(Figure 12)** The second house enhances the landscape. My studio is on the lower level, tucked under the terrace of the house where my family lives on the second floor. **(Figures 13 and 14)**

For a large exhibition space and a warehouse for a sanitary company in Carinthia, the southern part of Austria, we began the project with a very organised construction: a primary construction and a suspended secondary construction – a concrete structure with a huge glass roof. **(Figure 15)** The roof

11.
The Architect's House, Graz, Austria: Construction View of Terrace Frame. The site on which the studio and house stand lies directly below the summit of the Rosenberg on an old vineyard. The terracing of the vineyards is still recognizable and influenced the planning

12.
The Architect's House, Graz, Austria. The house lies above the office on the first natural terrace, length-ways along the second slope

13.
Below right
The Architect's House, Graz, Austria: The Studio Wall. The studio lies buried in the lowest part of the slope behind the 35 meter long and 5 meter wide, sloping glass wall. Counter-weights on pulleys move the 2x2 meter insulated glass panels (bonded to sliding hinges) like garage doors

Volker Giencke

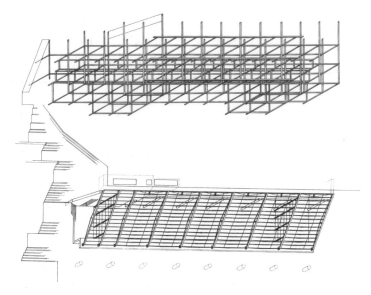

14.
The Architect's House (above) and Studio (below),
Graz, Austria. The primary structure is
constructed from 120 mm x 120 mm box section
steel on a 3m x 3m modular grid. The studio has
the cross-section of a trapezium with "rucksack"
which lies under the ground and opens onto the
studio space between concrete columns.
Extending in the direction of the ramp lie, one
after the other, the library, kitchenette, wash
room with WC and Atomic bomb shelter with
anteroom

15.
Below
Carinthia Warehouse: Interior View of roof
structure with suspended mirrors

structure is minimal with a few double suspended beams. The glass roof consists of 75-metre-long segments, which can be opened in two areas for natural ventilation. The construction of the glass roof is very subtle and very effective. It appears to be leaning on the rest of the structure. It is as if it comes out of the earth. **(Figure 16)**

From the street side, under the glass roof, there is a water basin and entry platform with a cascading staircase, sandwiched between two trusses, which leads from the exhibition floor to the second floor and passes by the entrance level. The exhibition of mirrors placed at different angles hangs from the roof. It is an exhibition of light.

As in the botanical greenhouse in Graz, the effect of the façade ever-changing in the light is what is interesting. The sunlight can be reflected by the glass roof and the shadows can be very strong. In the morning light the glass roof becomes very clear. During the afternoon, the light becomes softer. And, at twilight, the roof disappears. The disappearance of the architecture ends this essay, creating an artificial gravity that plays at supporting the organic subject.

**16.
Carinthia
Warehouse:
Exterior View**

Volker Giencke

7

William Katavolos

Organicism

In 1956 I founded the Guild for Organic Design in my studio on Great Jones Street, in New York City, in order to experiment with the concept of chemical architecture. This period culminated in a book called *Organics* which was published in Holland in the early 1960s by Steendrukkerej de Jong. The following extract from this represents my philosophy of organicism. **(Figure 1)**

A new architecture is possible through the matrix of chemistry. Man must stop making and manipulating, and instead allow architecture to happen. There is a way beyond building just as the principles of waves, parabolas, and plummet lines exist beyond the mediums in which they form. So must architecture free itself from traditional patterns and become organic. New discoveries in chemistry have led to the production of powdered and liquid materials which, when suitably treated with certain activating agents, expand to great size and then catalyze and become rigid. We are rapidly gaining the necessary knowledge of the molecular structure of these chemicals, together with the necessary techniques that will lead to the production of materials, which will have a specific program of behaviour built into them while still in the sub-microscopic stage. Accordingly it will be possible to take minute quantities of powder and make them expand into predetermined shapes such as spheres, tubes and toruses. Houses such as this would grow to certain sizes, subdivide or fuse for larger functions.

Great vaults would be produced with parabolic jets that catalyze on contact with the air, ceiling patterns are created like crystals, floors are

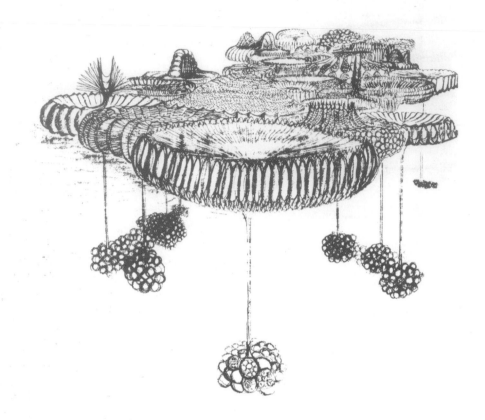

formed like corals, surfaces ornamented with stress patterns made visible. Exploding patterns of an instantaneous architecture of transformations, into desired densities, into known directions, for calculated durations.[1]

Some of my work of the moment is regarding a liquid villa. The liquid villa floats on compressed-air footings. The outer membranes are filled with fluid at less than atmospheric pressure and, in the process, create suction domes, vaults and arches within. Nitrogen gas is contained in the growing chambers, oxygen in the evacuated spaces and methane around the cliuus multrum waste-containers. **(Figures 2, 3, 4, 5 and 6)**. In an aqueous environment they would float. In desert surrounds, they are nonevaporative containers for potable water. **(Figures 7, 8 and 9)**

Note

1.   William Katavolos, *Organics*, Steendrukkerej de Jong (Hilversum), 1961. Reprinted in Ulrich Conrads (ed), *Manifestoes of 20th Century Architecture*, MIT Press (Cambridge MA), 1987, pp 163–4.

2.
The Liquid Villa,
2000, interior
rendering

3.
The Liquid Villa,
1999: Full-scale
models demonstrate
the inverted suction
dome and suction
column at less than
atmospheric
pressure

William Katavolos

4.
The Liquid Villa,
1999: Full scale
model of inverted
suction column

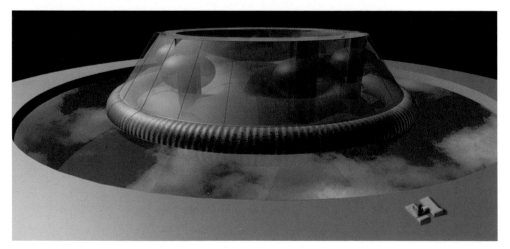

5.
The Liquid Villa,
2000, exterior
rendering

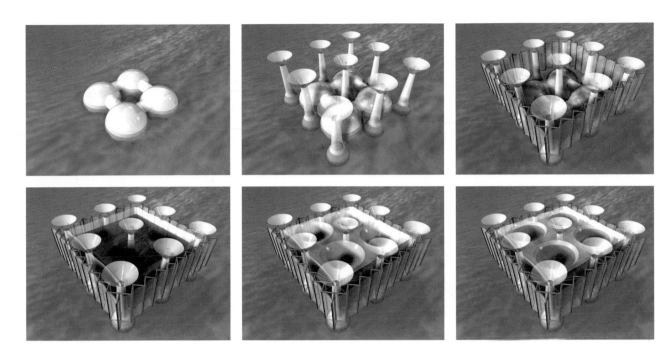

6.
The Liquid Villa,
2000: Study models
for expandable
floating
environments utilize
all of the villa
principles

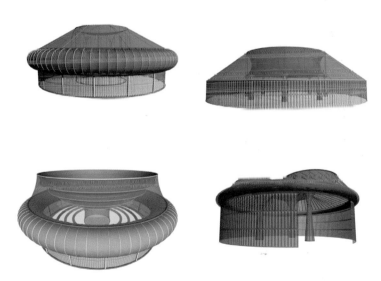

7.
The Liquid Villa, 2000: Examples of Low cost liquid villas
employ normal and tensile states of air and water. These units
are non-evaporative containers for potable water in desert
surrounds

William Katavolos

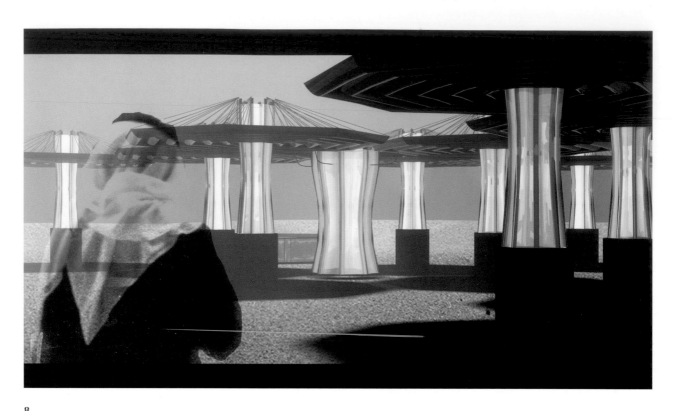

8.
The Liquid Villa, 2000: Non-evaporative containers for distillation and salinization using night sky radiation

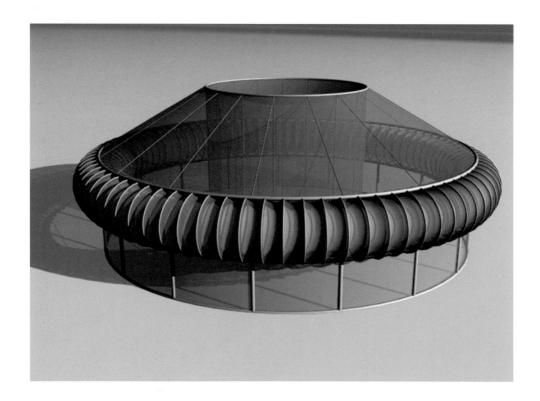

9.
The Liquid Villa 2000: Desert Installation

8

John Johansen

Organic Process

The word organic refers to nature and the characteristics of living organisms. In turn, an organism is a living being consisting of independent specialised organs which, in their interaction and interdependence, determine life processes. Certain of these processes of organisms may serve as man-made designs in architecture. They may be categorised as follows. Those pertaining to organisation are the circulatory and conductive and neural systems, which then serve as patterns for pedestrian and vehicular circulation, services distribution and communications. Those pertaining to the specialisation of functions are the separate body organs and the interrelation and interaction of those organs, which then may serve as an ordering device in the design of buildings as this helps to identify and qualify their purposes.

The use of bio-organisation as a model can be seen in my Oklahoma Theater Center, conceived in 1966 and completed in 1970. **(Figure 1)** Here we recognise the systematic disposition of architectural elements as 'organs', each with their specialised function, which in their programmed interrelation and interaction determine the activity of the centre. **(Figure 2)** We identify the three organs as the three theatres, each accompanied by smaller, supplementary, peripheral elements. These theatres are attached to a base, or calyx, and then to each other, by ramped tubes of pedestrian circulation. Colour coding distinguishes circulation for theatre guests, in red, from the confluence of public walks, in blue, and these from chilled water distribution pipes, high above, and air-conditioning elements, in black. All is interrelation, interaction and interdependency.

The performance aspects of an organism maintain its equilibrium in two forms. One form is in response and adaptation to the immediate environment by positive feedback, known as 'self-organisation'. A translation of this ability of organisms into architecture is found in the Citicorp Building in New York City, by the architect Hugh Stubbins and the engineer William Le Messurier. There the seismic monitoring of earthquake tremors by mechanical devices and the repositioning of the concrete tuned-mass damper as a counterweight maintain the building's stability. Other existing buildings employ hydraulic-powered jacks to maintain equilibrium in resistance to destabilising winds. In the British Pavilion at Seville designed by Nicholas Grimshaw, a kinetic self-operating shuttering system has been installed as protection against excessive sunlight.

The other variation of performance regarding equilibrium is the organism's maintenance of its own bodily functions. This is known as 'self-regulation'. The constant regulation of body temperature, blood flow, breathing, metabolism and neural communication sets a model from which our building design might well follow. The superb example of both regulatory and organisational performance is seen in the projected experiment, Green Building, of the late 1990s by the structural and environmental engineers Ove Arup of London, with the architect Jan Kaplicki. **(Figure 3)** Its odd shape is no whim of styling, but the consequence of some three years of computerised calculation, resulting in its self-organisation in response to changing environment, and its self-regulation of interior services and climate. **(Figure 4)** The double exterior membrane walls and central spaces direct a natural flow of temperature-controlled air and reflect natural light from the outside deep into its interior work spaces. This building, with its sensors and neural communications and performances, approaches the adaptive and symbiotic behaviours of the living organism. Some other applications of these principles are seen in models of several of my recent projects for the future: the Bubble Cluster, the Web, Flexstrut and the Metamorphic Capsule.

For the Cluster of 1985 I proposed a coalescence of inflated spherical membranes. These membranes are stabilised in balanced air pressures by air pumps, prompted by computerised messages from constant monitoring sensors in a form of cybernetic self-regulation. **(Figure 5)** They are also prompted by monitors to change their transparency to transluccncy to opacity, and to adjust their degrees of seasonal insulation so that they are self-organising. Movement through these bubbles would be by means of 'the levitator', a self-levelling capsule operating by a 'linear induction motor' on a serpentine monorail shown in red. The Cluster is a series of storings related functionally and also dependent on one another for support.

The Web from 1986, in which a new structure is suspended by cables from two cxisting urban towers, is an example of self-organisation. **(Figure 6)** In fierce winds the towers sway some 5 feet; but monitored, computerised jacks let out or pull in on the cables, whereby the suspended structure remains motionless. This would be a responsive building which, like a living creature, would adjust itself quickly to changing conditions in the environment that might threaten it.

Flexstrut could be described as movement and change in configuration. It is an effort to adapt organic performances to an artificial moving skeleton. **(Figure 7)** It is a framework similar to Buckminster Fuller's dome, but one in which every connecting node has flexibility, like the fingers of one's hand, and every strut can be controlled by motors to change its length. This allows for deformation of the framework from concave to convex, and changes in configuration. Thus by adaptation, this structure could accommodate various interior requirements. The theatre is such a structure for change. The Flexstrut Theater for Times Square demonstrates the possibility of changing the configuration to accommodate three different kinds of performance. **(Figures 8, 9 and 10)** One

John Johansen

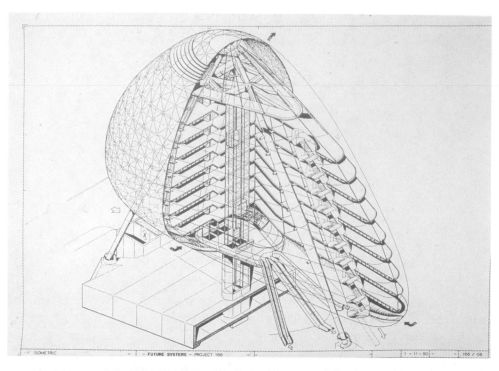

3.
Left
Green Building, 1997, by Jan Kaplicky and Future Systems (architects) with Ove Arup and Partners (engineers)

4.
Below
Green Building, 1997, by Jan Kaplicky and Future Systems (architects) with Ove Arup and Partners (engineers)

5.
The Cluster, 1985

John Johansen

6.
Above
The Web, 1989

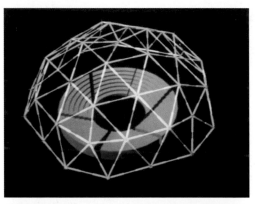

8.
Left
**Flexstrut Theater
as Theater-in-the-
Round**

7.
Above
Flexstrut Theater for Times Square 1993–4

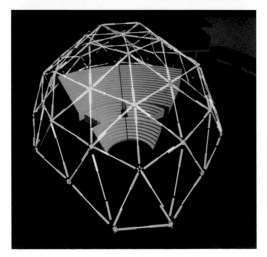

9.
Flexstrut Theater as Proscenium

10.
Flexstrut Theater as Ampitheatre

could imagine standing on the street looking up to watch the framework change slowly from one theatre to the other, from that of the matinée to that of a different evening performance. Although more expensive to build, it would be less expensive than three specialised theatres.

Another example of organic adaptability as performance would be the Metamorphic Capsule. It changes configuration by the manipulation of positive and negative electric forces acting between nodes on the capsule surface and corresponding nodes on the outer framework. **(Figures 11 and 12)** Its elastic membrane could change in light and colour as well, all variables being controlled by the occupant using a hand-held selector. The effects of the enclosure on the occupant are equally matched by the dictates and impulses of the occupant. This is then an example of 'cyberspace' in that architecture and occupant become one.

Ultimately, the most vital capacity of the organism is its ability to sustain life itself. In the man-made world of our future, research in nanotechnology, artificial intelligence and artificial life will advance our approach to this organic sustainability. Nanomolecular engineering is based on the concept of harnessing tiny molecular 'assembler robots'. Steven Levy, in *Artificial Life*, states that, 'robots, by definition, can be considered alive. For they grow, communicate and evolve.'[1] Recent research at Brandeis University has made progress in robot evolution and in simulated natural selection that has brought the man-made closer to evolution in nature. The psychologist James Hillman has written that, 'nanotechnology joins the realms of the organic with the inorganic, the models of biology and engineering.'[2] May we look forward to buildings which, by a form of 'natural selection', could improve their own design for increased performance and serviceability? In a generation or two, these present experiments will

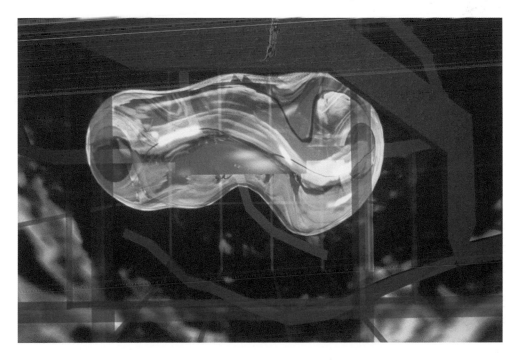

11.
Metamorphic
Capsule, 1991:
Exterior

John Johansen

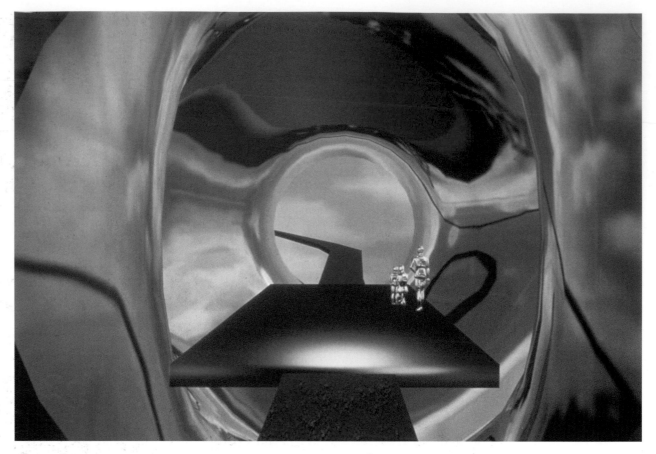

bring about a revolution in manufacturing and building. This is predicted by
Dr Eric Drexler, physicist and founding father of Wanotechnology. It is from the
related advanced research of the Foresight Institute that I draw my latest projects: the Growing House and the Growing High-Rise.

The house that will grow proceeds in the following sequence. **(Figures 13-
15)** A large vat is delivered from the factory to the building site. When the vat
is filled with the selected chemicals as bulk materials in liquid state, a code
or artificial DNA, known as the 'seed' is placed in it. The code will direct molecules to replicate themselves as a vast work force to build the house according
to software specifications. Roots will form in the vat, grow upwards and
outwards as grade beams reaching horizontally, then curving vertically to form
a branch system, with lattice infill and enclosing membranes. **(Figure 14)**
Interior platforms, partitions and stairways are supplied from nutrients in the
vat through what biologists refer to as a 'fibrovascular system'. Among the
various substances formed is one of pure carbon, some 50 times stronger
than steel and translucent, like diamond. Other substances would be flexible
elastic or like living muscles according to the 'sliding tissue principle'.
Membrane openings and closings will be possible as molecules can be prompted
by electrical charges to disengage and re-engage their linkages, or display
'morphability', in the parlance of physicists. **(Figure 15)** There are no actual
windows because the whole thing is window, which can be made opaque

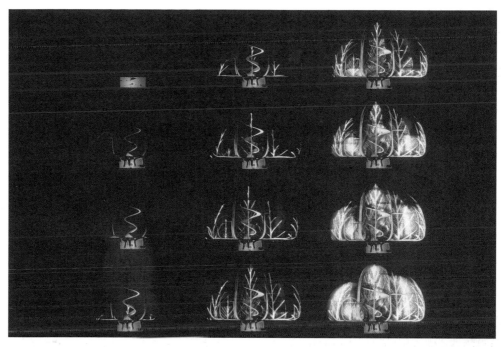

or transparent, open or closed, at any time you want by putting in such an electrical force.

Currently, I am designing a cantilevered bridge and a convertible museum, both of which are designed to grow.

To recapitulate, I have over my career observed and participated in four levels of development towards the organic: the appearance of the organic or of naturalism using biomorphic form by poetic or romantic metaphor; the organisation of

9.
Salmon Sleight of Hand
(a and b)

analogous points don't have to have a common cause. Similar structures arise for dissimilar purposes, and this is something to identify.

I am trying to relate this to architecture where, in a Situationist kind of way, there is also an appreciation of the connections and of the organising structure as a connecting. You can almost always put the word 'different' before layers. Layers are different. But a cell wall is shared from both sides. It is not a layer. In morphing you want something similar to the cell wall – that is, one membrane shared on both sides. You don't want the duplication of walls or layers so that the parts break apart, because then they are separate entities; then the analogy is lost and they become a collective. You need the boundary that is the shared wall, where the cells are not separate things that free-float but are continuities. This might not sound that profound a distinction but, in what I do and in the impression made, the distinction is central to the concept. The concept is connectivity of the elements, how they stick together. **(Figures 11a and 11b)**

10.
Face of Bodies
Morph

Tom Brigham

6.
Transforming Columns

7.
Wall System

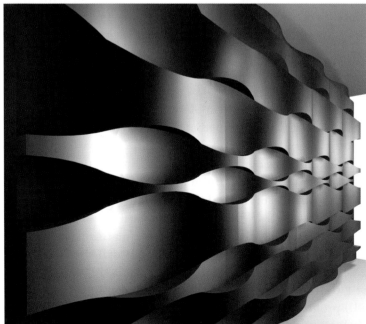

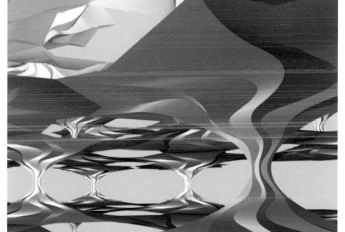

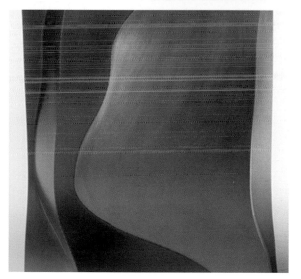

8.
Top
Ceiling System

9.
Above
Prototype Details for Architectural Surfaces

10.
Above
Wave Space Labyrinth

Haresh Lalvani

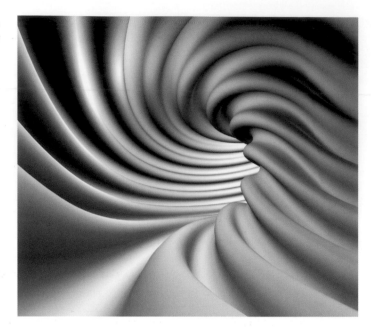

11.
Morphogenetic Pathway

for the beginning of *artificial genomics* as a parallel to biological genomics. As the morphological genome begins to be linked with physical morphogenesis (not digital, as in the case of 'artificial life') and, in time, automorphogenesis (self-replication),[22] the bridge between the artificial and the natural will begin to disappear. In this scenario of genomic architecture, architecture and biology will become one, reaching the upper limit definition of 'organic architecture'.

Notes

1. For origins of growing architecture, see William Katavolos, *Organics*, Steendrukkirj de Jong & Co (Hilversum), 1961; Vittorio Giorgini, 'Early Experiments in Architecture Using Nature's Building Technology' in H Lalvani (ed), *The International Journal of Space Structures*, 11: 1 and 2 (1997).
2. See, for example, K Eric Drexler, *Engines of Creation: The coming era of nanotechnology*, Anchor Books (New York), 1986, describing the future of building ultra-small and ultra-large objects atom by atom; Marvin Minsky, 'Will Robots Inherit the Earth?', *Scientific American* (October 1994), pp 109–113, where the author argues that they will, but as our 'mind-children' (using H Moravec's term); Ray Kurzweil, *The Age of Spiritual Machines*, Penguin Books (London), 1999, where the author predicts that by 2099 there will no longer be any clear distinction between humans and computers. On the software end, there is sufficient literature on artificial life describing attempts at re-creating life 'in silico'.
3. The paleontologist Stephen Jay Gould describes three possibilities in the landscape of imaginable lifeforms: 'can't work well', 'can't work at all' and 'just haven't been there yet' in 'Stretching to Fit', *The Sciences* (July/August 1998), pp 12–14.
4. Haresh Lalvani, 'Morphological Universe, Expanding the Possibilities of Design and Nature', unpublished manuscript, 1998, presented at the ACSA conference, 'Works of Nature: The Rhetoric of Structural Invention', Dalhousie University, Nova Scotia, October 1998.

5. This universe encompasses structures ranging from the microscopic to the macroscopic, from living to nonliving, chemical to biological, and those realised by humans and (eventually) by machines. See D'Arcy Thompson's classic *On Growth and Form*, Cambridge University Press (Cambridge), 1942.

6. The author has been working on this hyperuniverse since the late 1970s (first published in 1981, see note 7). The term 'morphological hyperuniverse' in this context was first used in print in the author's contribution to *Cyberspace: The world of digital architecture*, Images Publications (Australia), 2001, p 38.

7. Haresh Lalvani, *Structures on Hyper-Structures*, Lalvani (New York),1982; based on the author's doctoral dissertation *Multi-Dimensional Periodic Arrangements of Transforming Space Structures*, University of Pennsylvania (1981), University Microfilms (Ann Arbor), 1982.

8. Beginning with orderly structures like tilings, polyhedra, geodesic spheres, space-fillings, etc this universe is being continually mapped and extended by the author to be more encompassing. This extension includes a variety of curved structures as well as architectural and structural morphologies. The formal languages of selected architects (eg, Gaudi, Wright, Calatrava, to name a few we have been studying) provide fertile material for such mapping.

9. In 1971, the author began experimenting with various types of morphings, some related to D'Arcy Thompson's celebrated method of transformations, and others inspired by different types of growth in nature (eg, crystal growth) and move ment. During the mid-1980s, while Tom Brigham was experimenting with 'morphing' at the Computer Graphics Laboratory, New York Institute of Technology, the author, in collaboration with Robert McDermott and Patrick Hanrahan (also at CGL) was involved with a different type of continuous morphing, a structured morphing based on the reference in note 7.

10. The term 'morph-code' (or shape-code) raises the interesting question for biological form, whether such a code is embedded in the DNA sequences or whether biological form is purely the result of nongenetic factors (eg, physical or chemical forces). If yes, then mathematics in nature must be a by-product of the physics and chemistry of life, raising the intriguing question of how the biological genetic code triggers the formation of highly mathematical structures like the logarithmic spirals of seashells, to give one example.

11. A universal morphological coding would work at different scales of magnitude from the microscopic to the macroscopic. For example, the generative classification of transformational polyhedra embedded within the hyperuniverse would apply to the formal classification of crystal morphology. The corresponding sphere-packed configurations would apply to atomic arrangements in physics and chemistry. In principle, the morphological system of continually transforming space structures lends itself to modelling the constructions of kinetic nanoscale deployable structures (see also note 22).

12. It is possible that genetic codes other than DNA, RNA exist though none have been found so far. These (theoretically possible) codes would define the upper limit for all forms of life in the universe. The study of *all possible* biologies will fall within the domain of *hyperbiology*.

13. H. Lalvani, *Coding and Generating Islamic Patterns*, National Institute of Design, (Ahmedabad), 1982. Other articles by the author on this include: 'Pattern-Regeneration' in S Doshi (ed), *An Impulse to Adorn*, Marg Publications (Bombay) 1982; and 'Coding and Generating Complex Periodic Patterns', *Visual Computer* **5**, Springer-Verlag (Munich), 1989, pp 180–202.

14. H. Lalvani, 'Structures and Meta-Structures', *Symmetry of Structure*, International Society for the Inter-Disciplinary Study of Symmetry (Budapest), 1989.

Haresh Lalvani

15. In 1993, the author suggested the existence of 'skewed' fullerenes and hyper-fullerenes (higher dimensional analogs of fullerenes) as part of the 'periodic table of fullerenes' at his presentation at the 3rd International Conference on Space Structures, University of Surrey, 1993. Parts of this table were later published in the proceedings of the conference Katachi U Symmetry, Tsukuba University, Japan, 1994. Relating to note 11, it is interesting that the skewed fullerenes have the same underlying morphology as that of some of the spherical viruses with skewed icosahedral symmetry. The morphological hyperuniverse transcends scale at its root level, though each subuniverse will bring its own specificity.

16. In 1984, when Schectman et al at NIST (National Institute for Standards and Technology) reported the existence of a rapidly cooled alloy of manganese and aluminum based on icosahedral symmetry, till then denied in crystallography, a new class of natural nonperiodic structures (termed 'quasi-crystals') opened up. Interestingly, nonperiodic structures were independently discovered in different fields: mathematics, physics, crystallography and architecture. The author's independent work during the period 1981–5, and subsequently, was amongst those within the field of architecture along with the works of Baer and Miyazaki.

17. This particular example, related to the Penrose tiling, is a projection from four dimensions. The dimensionality of the structure increases with the extent of subdivision of the surface and results in increasing irregularity.

18. This roof concept was developed in 2001 in collaboration with Maria Sevely and Archronica architects on their project for a pharmaceutical company.

19. US Patent No. 6,341,460.

20. A major effort is currently being planned for assembling the tree of life to construct a phylogeny of the 1.7 million described species of life.

21. Francis S Collins and Karin G Jegalian, 'Deciphering the Code of Life' in *Editors of Scientific American*, *Understanding the Genome*, Warner Books (New York), 2002, p 37.

22. The idea of using morph-coded designs of Drexler's nanotech 'assemblers' and 'replicators' (cited in note 2) is a more direct application of morphogenomics. Morph-coded shapes (and materials) that change from one to another using transformation pathways within the hyperuniverse can be constructed using Drexler's proposal for building atom by atom. On a related note, the author, in the early 1970s in an unpublished paper, had suggested achieving 'automorphogenesis' using genetically engineered bacteria as an alternative method of self-replication that relies on a biological process of building.

Acknowledgements

The author wishes to thank the School of Architecture, Pratt Institute, for its support of the Center for Experimental Structures where the author is a co-director. Various individuals have contributed generously to this project in different ways over the years. Their tireless efforts are gratefully acknowledged. Computer modelling: Neil Katz at Skidmore, Owings and Merrill, New York City; Computer rendering: Mohamad Al-Khayer and Ajmal Aqtash; Product development at Milgo: Bruce Gitlin and Alex Kveton; Photography at Milgo: Robert Wrazen. The author also wishes to thank the biophysicist Loren Day for his constructive remarks on the paper.

The project AlgoRhythm Structures (with Milgo/Bufkin) is currently being funded by NYSTAR (New York State Technology and Academic Research, 2002–3). Some of the ideas in this article were published in the author's 'Meta Architecture', *Architectural Design* (Sept/Oct 2000), and republished in Giuseppa di Cristina (ed), *Architecture and Science*, Wiley-Academy, 2001.

1 1

Todd Dalland

Lightness and Movement

Lightweight and flexible construction materials have enabled the 'degravitation' of buildings. Solar energy, waste recycling, rainwater collection and wireless communications have liberated them from sites 'on the grid'. Standardisation, prefabrication, containerisation and semitrailers enable truly lightweight buildings to pack up economically and 'travel' from site to site with their autonomous infrastructures, as needed.

Ten years ago we developed some elements of tensile structure technology and conventional steel framing into a concept for a permanent Fabric Skyscraper. **(Figure 1)** We didn't have a client or an end-user – just an idea to make a curtain wall that would be beautiful, light, economical and with relatively few linear feet of waterproofing joints. Several years ago, a 60-storey fabric curtain wall was built at the Arabian Tower Hotel in Dubai.

A year ago, we developed some elements of tensile structure technology, construction scaffolding, technology and event-industry infrastructure technology into a concept for a Recyclable, Portable, Fabric Skyscraper. **(Figure 2)** Again, we had no client or end-user or even an end-use – just an idea to demonstrate something that was technically possible for us. How long will it be before someone actually finds a use for this idea?

The Recyclable, Portable, Fabric Skyscraper is a 12-storey building with 48 space rental suites, intended for temporary use on vacant urban sites for durations of six months to three years. It has a total construction schedule of six weeks.

Many people consider the fabric-clad scaffolding structures that temporarily envelop the facades of so many buildings in our cities to be a necessary evil

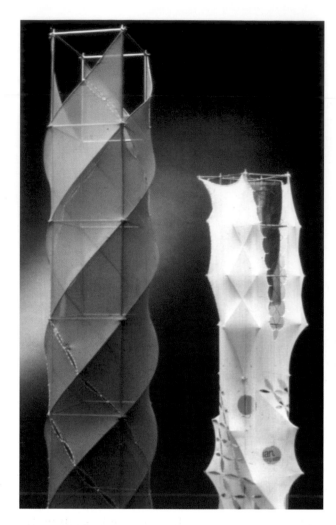

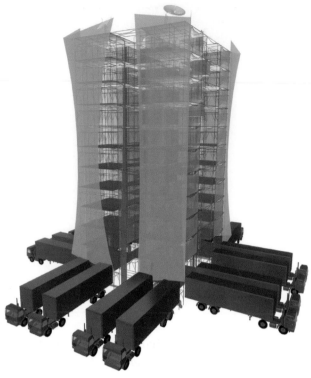

1.
Left
Fabric Skyscraper Study

2.
Above
Recyclable Portable Fabric Skyscraper

of building repair and maintenance. We consider them to be temporary, usable, rentable real estate. In fact, why not create an entire building with scaffolding, standard clip-on floor planks, standard clip-on construction-industry elevators, stackable event-industry modular toilets and a double-layered fabric curtain wall? **(Figure 3)** In our concept for this new, occupiable, layer of urban fabric all the infrastructure – power supply, water and waste lines, and HVAC – are housed in event-industry truck trailers that occupy the ground floor of the building. All services and utilities are risered-up with clip-on, flexible conduits and ducts. These components are standard, modular and reusable – making the entire building recyclable. Most of its components can be reinventoried and reconfigured on other sites, wherever and whenever they are needed.

The building's proportions in terms of its width-to-height ratio are determined so that the building can be assembled on a flat site without any foundations penetrating the ground's surface. The overturning moments from full design wind-loading are resisted by the building's self-weight and temporary ballast added on the lower floors.

It's beautiful; it can occupy almost any site; and it only occupies the site when it is needed. Have Skyscraper, will travel. The building has been approved

3.
Double Layered Fabric Curtain Wall over Scaffolding

by the Department of Really Fast Buildings and requires a Visa for international travel. Slow buildings move to the right lane. . .

Frei Otto and others taught us the core values of lightweight structures: forms in nature as the aesthetic ideal, materials selected for high-tensile strength properties, minimal surfaces stressed in tension like soap films in nature, materials that are lightweight, flexible and often translucent, surfaces and spaces that are doubly curved like saddle surfaces and domes, rigid supports configured as masts and shells in pure axial compression with no bending, and the conservation of material, energy and mass. The human skull, for example, starts out as a soft, thin, lightweight, tensile material that is internally pressurised to its final size – in and out of the womb – and then hardened to become a strong, thin shell structure.

Archigram and others showed us that advances in technology cause societal changes faster than ever, so our buildings should be technically savvy, flexible enough to adapt to changing programmes, and reinvented in ever-shortening cycles.

Thesis:

- Walls and roof components should be lightweight, flexible, multilayered membranes stressed in tension.
- Rigid supports should be modular systems that can fold up and disassemble readily.
- Infrastructure and foundations should be portable and not penetrate the ground surface.

These buildings shall be called OttoGrams TM®©

William Katavolos and others have pointed out that buildings are moving from mass to membrane, and that a building's skin is its environmental filter. We believe that a building's skin should be made of multiple, lightweight, flexible, doubly curved membranes stressed in tension with as many membranes as are necessary for a particular site and function; each membrane performing a different task – structure, thermal insulation, waterproofing, etc.

We are working with Honeywell on the design and engineering of a small building addition to be deployed in outer space. It is an exit/entry module for two fully suited astronauts to use to perform EVAs (extra-vehicular activities) on the new space shuttle for NASA. It is a pneumatic structure with 12 layers of membranes, two layers of air beams and one layer of pneumatic muscles. **(Figure 4)** The outermost material lay-up of six layers of flexible or folding membranes performs the functions of micrometeoroid protection (armour against organic and man-made debris in Earth orbit) and temperature insulation (temperatures range from -200°F to +200°F). The innermost material lay-up

Todd Dalland

Here are two examples of these principles:

- Each summer the Carlos Moseley Pavilion for the Metropolitan Opera and the New York Philharmonic goes to 19 sites in the five bouroughs – with five, fully loaded, custom-designed semitrailers – and sets up in four hours with no foundations. It's an instant building. 'Tectonics' include truck wheels, tail lights and crane booms instead of posts, lintels and Ionic columns: a new language. The remote-speaker towers are wire-less and accommodate an audience of 100,000 people with delayed, blended sound. Truck or building? Machine or building? **(Figure 8)**
- The Time for Peace Pavilion is a travelling museum with its own power generation and infrastructure – and toilets, offices and concessions. Everything is above ground so you step through temporary thresholds over the utility wiring, piping and ducting. Of the eight trucks, four com-prise the building and four service it. The vertical support A-frames hinge down to lie on top of the trailers for travel. **(Figure 9)** At the site the A-frames hinge up; the walls of the trucks fold down and out to become the floors; and the fabric membranes pull up and out to become the roof and walls. The building floor height is the truck floor height. **(Figure 10)**

Norman Foster and others have encouraged us to look at the design and con-struction process for buildings in the way industrial and product designers look at their design and fabrication processes for products and standardised struc-tures. Our 'products' are often lightweight structures with thin skins stretched over slender supports, creating large, open, naturally lit, universal spaces – with industrial strength utility packages, strategically placed networks of pipes, wires and ducts spun through the skins, and free-plan partial-height walls. **(Figure 11)**

All components are prefabricated in controlled factory environments where higher accuracy on tolerances for construction and installation can be obtained.

8.
Carlos Moseley
Travelling Music
Pavilion with
Speaker Towers

Photo credit:
Jeff Goldberg, © Esto

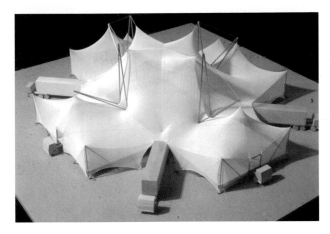

Conservation of energy can be optimised through reduction of weight and materials. Activities can be optimised through ordering and reduction of scheduling. Machine-like efficiency of function, structure and mechanical systems can be obtained through the optimisation of feedback loops over the life of the 'product'.

Design of custom castings, extrusions and connectors for mass production is part of the design team's responsibility. **(Figures 11 and 12)** We design and engineer some of the connection details for lightweight and deployable buildings, particularly prefabricated ones, in our model shop. They start out as wood and clay models and eventually become castings in aluminium and steel. We shape them so they use the least amount of material possible, and initially place the material only where it's needed functionally. We exploit the best and highest structural characteristics of a particular material appropriate for a certain application, and use the least amount of that material that is structurally possible. **(Figure 13)** *Structure is one of the major determinants of the form of a building.*

Happold and others have encouraged us to integrate architects and engineers in the building design process, particularly in lightweight structures where nature teaches us that: form is structure; forces naturally travel in optimal shapes and patterns; and forces and forms are material specific. These are the shapes and patterns from nature that designers should manipulate to make spaces and buildings. *The resulting beauty is appropriate.*

'It is structurally immoral to make the forces in buildings behave in unnatural ways.' Ted Happold

The next logical extension is the integration of the mechanical engineer into the process of designing good 'weather' inside the building – or comfort zones – naturally optimised to the point where the internal environmental design becomes a major determinant of the form of the building. This logic goes on to include the integration of material suppliers, fabricators, erectors and building maintainers with the initial building design team, with each of them contributing building-form determinants. *The resulting beauty is appropriate.*

We maintain the notion that integrated design-engineering work – whether as lead designers or as consultants to lead designers – is more valuable than just design work, or just engineering work. More valuable than segregated design and engineering work.

Todd Dalland

We are trying to learn more about ourselves and the world and to create glimpses of the future of buildings and society; and we believe that the key to our endeavour is the embracing of emerging technologies and the humanising of them, to both anticipate and influence possibilities for appropriate beauty in the future.

Lightness, flexibility, movement, recyclability and minimum expenditure of energy are unmistakable as increasingly important elements of building design.

12. Eureka Clay Model Plate Fitting, FTL, architect

11. Clay Models for Castings of Tent Connections, FTL, architect

13. Detail Plate of AT&T Global Olympic Pavilion for the Atlanta Olympics, FTL, architect

1 2

Mahadev Raman

Environmental Flow

I am going to discuss conventional buildings, but ones that draw certain references to organic issues and the environment. The first is Kansai Airport, Osaka, whose main hall is a kilometre long with a curved roof that draws references from organic animals. **(Figure 1)** In an airport, even at an early stage, many issues are defined by the programme, such as passenger volume and security, and there are already a huge number of restrictions as a result. The challenge becomes, as in many buildings, the main space, which in this case is the check-in area. The design process was a collaboration between Renzo Piano, my mentor Tom Barker and Peter Rice. They sat down and wondered how they might go about identifying an appropriate shape for this large space and in the process asked how they would air-condition it. **(Figures 2a and b)** Conventionally there would be ducts all over the place with weight that must be supported by the roof. They considered an alternative – a single large jet of air that moves 80 metres across the entire hall. Once they had decided on the jet, the movement of temperature and of air velocities, the way air is displaced defined the shape of the roof. **(Figure 3)** Everything about the roof came out of the physical calculations about the trajectory of this jet of air. The reference to the spine emerged from the structure that supports the roof between two points. A number of ribs assembled altogether form the space. **(Figure 4)** There was a certain literalism in the references from nature and from organics to the form of the building. **(Figure 5)**

The Phoenix Courthouse by Richard Meier is a more conventional, Modernist architecture, a rectangular building for a city block in an L-shape of

1.
Kansai International Airport, Osaka, Japan, 1994, Aerial view. Renzo Piano Building Workshop, Architects, Ove Arup & Partners, engineers

2.
Kansai Airport Air Distribution System Diagram (a) Digital Model of environment in summer (b), Ove Arup & Partners, engineers

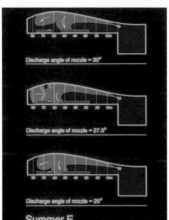

Discharge angle of nozzle = 30°

Discharge angle of nozzle = 27.5°

Discharge angle of nozzle = 25°

Summer E

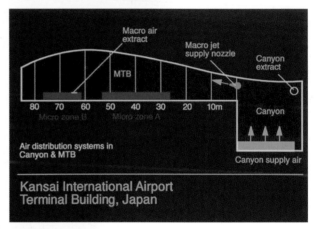

Macro air extract

Macro jet supply nozzle

Canyon extract

MTB

80   70   60   50   40   30   20   10m

Micro zone B   Micro zone A

Canyon

Air distribution systems in Canyon & MTB

Canyon supply air

Kansai International Airport Terminal Building, Japan

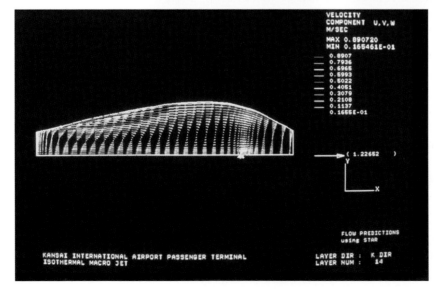

VELOCITY COMPONENT U,V,W M/SEC
MAX 0.890720
MIN 0.165461E-01

0.8907
0.7936
0.6965
0.5993
0.5022
0.4051
0.3079
0.2108
0.1137
0.1655E-01

(1.22662)

FLOW PREDICTIONS using STAR

KANSAI INTERNATIONAL AIRPORT PASSENGER TERMINAL ISOTHERMAL MACRO JET

LAYER DIR : K DIR
LAYER NUM : 14

3.
Kansai Airport, Preliminary Air Movement Profile

4.

Top Left

Kansai International Airport, Osaka, Japan, 1994, Interior view. Renzo Piano Building Workshop, Architects, Ove Arup & Partners, Engineers

Photo credit: Ishida Shunji

5.

Top Right

Kansai International Airport, Osaka, Japan, 1994, Interior view. Renzo Piano Building Workshop, Architects, Ove Arup & Partners, Engineers

Photo credit: Yotaka Kinumaki

spaces around a large atrium. **(Figure 6)** So far, none of this has any reference to nature. However, the extreme situation of a glass box in a desert, with so many hot days, air-conditioning loads etc, also represented a great opportunity with regard to environmental design. **(Figure 7)** By analysing the climate of Arizona and understanding how the glass box might act with the high temperature and low humidity, we managed to understand how such spaces behave and how the building would interact with the environment. **(Figure 8)** We came up with a solution that is entirely natural and mostly passive without air-conditioning. Studying the relation of the building to the sun, we developed a series of shading devices that prevent the sun penetrating the space. On the north, the glass is clear because, although it's exposed, the sun rarely shines on that face. Then we identified zones of natural ventilation. **(Figure 9)** The plan shows the huge opportunity for evaporative cooling from roofing, a natural method that has been used for centuries. The air comes in from the top. We used shading devices over the entire ceiling below the roof to absorb energy from the sun. **(Figure 10)** These get hot enough to fry an egg, and generate hot air – hotter than outside. As the hot air escapes at the top, more air is drawn in. It comes in with such a velocity that it shoots across the space and, at this point, is sprayed with water so that it evaporates instantly – atomises. You can see a cloud hovering above you as it evaporates. The water cools the air, which becomes humid and denser and descends in a cascade where it generates comfortable corridor conditions. You get a blast of cold air at the bottom and an overflow of 15 feet above ground level.

In contrasting the two projects, you might think of the Kansai shape as being more organic in the literal sense of spinal columns and movements of air but, in terms of the user's experience, it's a static experience. Once you are in the building it doesn't matter what happens outside. Cloudy or not, its internal environment is isolated and uniform. **(Figure 11)** Yes, in summer there is one condition and in winter another, slightly cooler, one but the user experience within the building is constant throughout. Kansai is a fine monumental and functional fulfilment of programme, but it's always the same space. The air velocity is always the same. The air temperature is always the same. The

Mahadev Raman

6.
Federal Building and US Courthouse, Phoenix, Arizona, 2000, Model, Richard Meier and Partners, architects, Ove Arup and Partners, engineers

Photo credit: Scott Frances, © Esto

7.
Federal Building and US Courthouse, Phoenix, Arizona, 2000, Interior View. Richard Meier and Partners, architects, Ove Arup and Partners, engineers

Photo credit: Scott Frances, © Esto

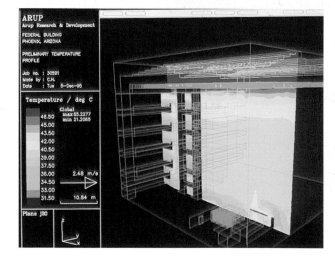

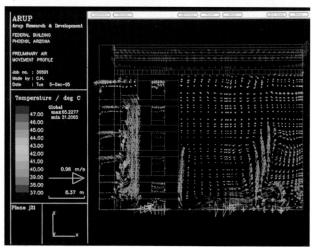

8.
Preliminary Temperature Profile of Phoenix Courthouse, Ove Arup & Partners, engineers

9.
Preliminary Air Movement Profile of Phoenix Courthouse, Ove Arup & Partners, engineers

10.
Federal Building and US Courthouse, Phoenix, Arizona. Roof of Courthouse. Richard Meier and Partners, architects

Photo credit: © Esto

Mahadev Raman

Phoenix courthouse is a box, a human imposition on the landscape; but, in terms of the user experience, it is dynamic. **(Figure 12)** The velocity of the air is dependent on solar radiation. On a bright sunny day you might feel the air move across the space. The temperature fluctuations are such that in winter you actually might be a bit chilly. There are few cloudy days in Phoenix, but when there are there is a noticeable difference in the way the air moves in the space and in the quality of light. Of course, day and night are also quite different. The building interacts with the environment in a more organic, more responsive, way than Kansai and this response becomes a direct experience to the user.

11.
Main Hall Kansai Airport.
Renzo Piano Buiding
Workshop, architects

Photo credit:
Ishida Shunji

12.
Interior Night View,
Courtroom, Phoenix
Courthouse. Richard
Meier and Partners,
architects

Photo credit: © Esto

13

Panellists: Tom Brigham, Todd Dalland, Deborah Gans, John Johansen, William Katavolos, Zehra Kuz, Mahadev Raman

Panel Discussion

Deborah Gans: It is a special honour for me to introduce this panel composed of people who, with the exception of Tom Brigham, have taught at Pratt. (Maybe we can get Tom to teach there too). I was privileged to serve as a departmental chairman at Pratt for several years, during which time I became familiar with individual achievements of the faculty and also their shared culture of the organic. It is a tradition of great historical depth at Pratt. When I asked Bill Katavolos where I should begin this history, suggesting perhaps with his teacher at Pratt in the industrial design department, Eva Zeisel, he said: 'No, it starts before that with my teacher Paul Nelson – no before that with my teacher Frederick Kiesler.' These panellists have developed a shared culture over at least 30 years, not in a single set of ideas but as a dynamic set of propositions that continue to evolve and change with the times.

The subject of this panel is the operation of the 'so called' organic object. It takes up Ahmet's discussion of the organism's persistent organisation in space and time that resists entropy. The preceding talks have explored the occurrence of change within the continuity of such an object. We have seen form finding and transformation in genetic, molecular, material and architectural modes that are generated internally as well as in response to external factors.

I am of two minds. Maybe we could start the panel discussion by talking about the weather – or else skip the pleasantries and talk about decay. Todd, would you mind following up on Mahadev's talk about the weather? How do you go about shaping a dynamic internal environment within your fabric skins?

Todd Dalland: I love Mahadev's design ideas and design technique of using computer software to model the way gas at different temperatures moves through space so you can define where the comfort zones align and then adjust them to where people are, and then let those criteria give the building form. There is a lot of software out there with knowledge of structural properties and material properties built into it; but I have never seen one that integrates all three – structural, material and climatic properties – in the one software where all the criteria work together to form the shape of the building. You are talking about finding form.

There is one mistake in understanding I don't want people to make, namely, that we are slaves to this software. Every step of the way, we are evaluating form as it's being processed. Sometimes we will stop the structural software from being 100 per cent efficient because it is creating something that isn't allowing the truck to drive through, or the sun to come in; or it is creating something ugly. So we stop it and manipulate it. The same thing with the weather. We are using these great tools to help us to discover sensible forms but we are still responsible for making the poetry.

Mahadev Raman: Just as we heard that in our lifetime we won't see a computer that can identify a thumb, or that image, the same goes for the tools we use. As Todd said about his design process, the tools don't take over; they allow you to understand, quantify and perhaps optimise certain things that as a designer you are trying to integrate within the building. Each one of my CFD (computational fluid dynamic) images of temperature and so on is for one instant in time; and to produce one such analysis at this moment, with a very powerful silicon graphics computer, takes up to about 36 hours. If you were to expand that formula into what you would actually need in the future, namely the integration of the environmental side with structural issues and the time-dependent behaviour of the environment, you are looking at a hundredfold increase in computing power. This is not with us just yet. It is as if all the theoretical framework, all the equations, all the methods, all the mathematics

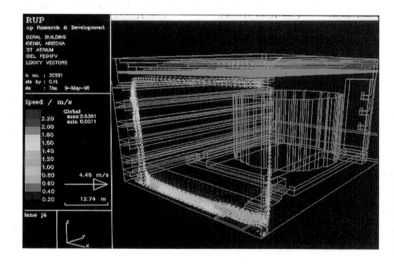

1.
Phoenix Courthouse, 2000, Preliminary Digital, Model of air dynamics. Ove Arup & Partners, engineers, Richard Meier and Partners, architects

are understood; but there isn't any program powerful enough to integrate them as a supertool. Even when we have the supertool, it won't go off by itself and produce excellence.

William Katavolos: Engineers aren't famous for collectively perfected systems. They like to bracket things. The lighting engineer and plumber won't be in on the same day. But here, today, you are beginning to see a collective perfection of building. What Todd and Mahadev are doing over there is almost neo-nature, in the Goethe mould. 'You are creating a new planet', Moholy said. 'Architecture is moving from mass towards motion', not just mass towards membrane. You are moving mass towards membrane and motion both.

The increasing sophistication of the computer software is very important. Studio Max, which gives you the instant volume of a changing shape, is enormously valuable to my work. I remember 30 years ago when the only purpose of the computer was to change the shape of an ounce, for perfume companies who wanted new bottles. Finally we have our hands on this kind of programming. What I want to see is the constant reshaping of water in my system and the creation and shaping of kidneys, livers and lungs. Keisler and I had an argument at the Museum of Modern Art one day. I said to him, 'For Chrissake, enough of the endless house, how about its kidney and liver. When are you going to fill this thing up?' He got very mad at me and said, 'Goddamn it, I'll build the egg, you build the chicken.' So I have been building the chicken ever since.

Matthew Jelacic (audience): Is the mathematics used to model the fluid dynamics of air at Kansai similar to that used to model evaporating water for the tents, because the two seem formally similar in many ways? Is it the same software?

Raman: You can't move the software for different applications at this time; but, as you delve into the fundamentals of engineering, you find that the equations governing them are very much the same.

Brent Porter (audience): Bill, I am interested in the applicability of medical technology to your architecture. A Texas doctor is actually grafting a living heart when it's pulsing. Is any of this technology being incorporated?

Katavolos: This is where it all came from. Membrane research came from blood dialysis units. They didn't know what to do with it. Donnoucos developed the first membrane for General Electric, first in heart dialysis then in reverse osmosis. It was an extraordinary thing, but they couldn't sell it. Little by little, the vocabulary was creeping into the architecture we have today. Between the military and the medical, we get everything.

Dan Buscescu (audience): Tom, in your presentation you made an opposition between an organ and culture. Then you referred to a cognitive module. What do mean by this term cognitive module?

Tom Brigham: It's like a built-in, as with the language instinct. These things we take for granted as being present, which are visible to us, are actually quite structured in advance. Exercising these structures in a playful way is interesting.

Buscescu: Where does it come from?

Brigham: I am told it's a product of evolution.

Buscescu: It sounds ambiguous. It comes from the organ or organism but it could come from culture. In a way, in the case of the cognitive module, culture has interfered with the organism.

Brigham: I would say that it is part of defining the organism in a prevailing culture and context. If you are in the woods, it is useful to be able to pick out a stalking lion quickly without first having to evaluate each piece of it to determine it's a lion – at which point it is too late. We live in this world which, in terms of what physics tells us, is filled with illusion. We take these illusions as the primary constituents of reality because they are our cognitive modules and our grip. Think of colour – it is a band within a spectrum. X-rays would have colour if we had cognitive modules operating in those parts of the spectrum. There is no physical reason why colours should be seen in one part of the spectrum and not in another. These are our illusions: organising structure, seeing entities and pulling them out of the environment. Cognitive modules, like humans in general, are competing or collaborating cultural entities.

**2.
Boston Harborlights
Pavilion, 1994, FTL**

Photo credit:
David Woods

Gans: It seems to me that Todd's architecture is purposefully unresolved in its capacity to organise. Because it is both infrastructural and ephemeral it has a vacillating presence and power within culture. It seems to me, Todd, that you are very concerned with the way this culture of tents could organise us in dialogue with the constituent permanencies, like infrastructure, built by communities over time.

Dalland: We are discussing a project for Grant Park in Chicago that will be a series of spaces for different functions and that will be removable, will come and go. We will build the infrastructure. It will be the hard-scape of the park. Water supply, electrical supply will be in place. So here we have a building in a park that is half permanent, half temporary, half hard and half soft. When we worked for the Olympics in Atlanta, we were building for several million people and one-third of the buildings existed, one-third were new permanent structures and one-third were temporary – a few millions of square feet. We would, in some cases, take existing hard buildings and add temporary buildings all around them so that they could be effectively bigger for the period of a month. You can imagine, in a city, doing something similar, with buildings that come and go. Where there is a plaza around the building, you could have temporary buildings just when you need them with the infrastructure and foundations built in. You can imagine roofs that come and go over plazas, as buildings for interim functions. You can imagine, by building infrastructure and foundations and then using light and flexible materials, an urban situation that is a bit more ephemeral.

John Johansen: Even the infrastructure is impermanent if you look at it broadly. I am thinking of the operations of the human being and the term dynamic stability. We all operate on this principle. All our tissues change within one to 14 years. If it is the bone or brain, it's a long time. If it's skin, it's immediate. If I came upon any of you in an average of seven years no same tissue, in principle, would be there. No tissue is permanent. What is permanent is you, an idea, an organisation of tissue. Even the infrastructure goes as well. Everything is dispensable. This is a more accurate way of speaking of permanence.

Katavolos: I think the question of the difference between the temporary and permanent is a good one. It gets to the heart of a lot of problems. In the Shinto temple that is re-erected every 22 years exactly as it was, we have a perpetual structure. The Parthenon was put up once; it's permanent. My own architecture, if you pull the plug, it is gone. It is perpetual not permanent, but it's not temporary.

John Lobell (audience): The implication of John's statement, that although the cells are changing there is a 'you', is one of essence. I would say that the difference between Corb, Mies, humanist architecture and this architecture of today is one of essence. Do you have thoughts on how human beings operate differently as ideas now?

Lalvani: Simple answer. Commerce. Companies want the biggest bang for their buck. We tried to get a toy out to introduce the idea of the fourth dimension to children. It took three years before it was dropped. Companies don't want to spend that kind of time. They also want products that move off the shelves quickly and lend themselves to television promotion. I was surprised to learn that a major company marketing Scrabble, incidentally a game developed by an architect, said they would probably reject it if it was presented to them today.

Gans: Are you saying capitalism resists complexity?

Lalvani: Yes, in a sense. I am saying that it's not so easy to bridge the gap in practice. The fluidity and the organicism that we speak of in architecture must apply to commerce as well. We will need an organic form of capitalism. This means fluidity in manufacturing and distribution as well. I think, in time, this will happen. Mass customisation, which essentially deals with designing complexity, will happen sooner than we think.

Katavolos: We have had 80 years of John Dewey, of learning by doing, and it doesn't work. The only thing that works is learning by undoing. You have to undo what your parents have already done. You have to undo the damage. You can't be force-fed what you have found out. You can't shove water up a tree; it has to be sucked up from the roots. Education has to totally change.

Theo David (audience): Your presentations expose that, as science and medicine give us longer life spans, we are making architectural structures with shorter life spans, in reverse of our monumental urges of 3000 years ago. I am wondering what this shift will do to the human psyche.

Gans: Theo's question recalls Bill's distinction between the perpetual and the permanent. It's a similar question, but focused on decay. In Jhedda, Mali, the decay of the mosque is the perpetuator of culture. Because the mosque is made out of stucco and the climate is harsh, it decays every year and is restuccoed every year by the community. The decay of the mosque differs from the Shinto temple, which is ritualistically burned and reassembled, in that it is a 'natural' consequence of an environmental situation. As Ahmet reminded us, the only law of thermodynamics that has time in it is entropy. The mosque's decay has entropy's linear dynamic of time interrupted by a periodic act of culture.

Raman: This issue of decay takes place in all buildings and should be a design factor in all buildings. Not just decay in the general sense, but specific terms for particular elements. In the typical building, whether modern or ancient Greek, there were really only two elements: art works and the basic structure. In a contemporary building there are a whole host of elements that decay over different time scales. If you look at the structure, concrete and steel most usually, they last a very long time – long enough to far outlive the designers, providing there isn't a catastrophic event. But the roofing materials and the facade might decay over a 50-year life span. The electrical and mechanical systems last 25 to 35 years. When you come to the newest systems like cabling for IT, the hardware is on a two-year cycle; the software is decaying on a six-month cycle. So decay is inherent in the structure. The recognition of different rates and cycles is important

David: As John Dewey put it, the renewal is also part of the design. And as John Johansen said, renewal is part of the way we as organisms have been designed. I would like to distinguish between that cycle of natural decay and repair and Bill's act of pulling the plug as well. One is natural the other is willful.

Brigham: Relating Theo's concern with architectural change and decay to the information age, my perspective is that today people expect information to be itself transforming, even in terms of their own selves. In the 1950s, if you were describing a guy with a certain personality you would call him eccentric; today you would say that he should go into therapy and change himself. We have a different attitude towards the stability of information. These portable buildings, even if they are permanently installed, are especially welcome because people think they can come back next year and change them. They are available for change. People are comfortable with the idea that maybe they'll just change their architecture so that they won't get bored, as opposed to the Greeks who were fighting for permanence.

Johansen: As regards impermanence, in molecular engineering they will employ 'assemblers' that build, repair and keep a structure renewed. On other occasions, they will employ 'disassemblers' that reduce the structure to basic material and prepare the material for recycling. Not unlike the NASA proposal for mining on Mars. That is rather beautiful.

4.
Kansai Airport, 1994, Interior.
Renzo Piano Building Workshop,
architects, Ove Arup and Partners,
engineers

Photo credit: Ishida Shunji

Gans: Haresh, you wrote that while architects tend to think of the fourth dimension as time, in your coding you try to translate higher temporal dimensions back into space. Isn't your genetic universe of form getting rid of decay? You are taking the temporal element as spatial or geometric. What does that do to the idea of transformation, evolution or of decay in the other direction.

Lalvani: This isn't quite what I meant. I wanted to say that, in the epoch of Einstein we had the space-time idea in which three-dimensional space was linked with time as the fourth dimension; but we also had the fourth dimension as space. The Einsteinian idea was so powerful that it dominated culture and architecture. Today it is more widely known that space can have any number of dimensions. Whether physical space can only have three is a question; some physicists have suggested evidence of higher dimensions in recent years, albeit at an ultra-small scale. But mathematical space can have any number of dimensions; and time can then always be added to it – as an additional dimension. So a multidimensional structure can still be talked about as evolving in time. I think the real question here is: is architecture like physics or mathematics at its most fundamental level? My answer would be: it is both. The closer we get to the bottom, the more the distinction between physics and mathematics ceases to be.

Katavolos: Einstein was a frequent visitor at Falling Water, as a friend of ol' man Kaufmann. Wright put up the first pier and he consciously opened it up to become a room, which Louis Kahn takes credit for. And then Wright raised the house and slid the continuous concrete tray through the stone, which is discontinuous, and slotted the glass so it was allowed to pass through. Every element passes by each other without touching. All materials and dimensions pass through – length, width, depth and time. This is the closest thing to space-time with time as the fourth dimension that there is in architecture. It's the most extraordinary structure in the world. You're right Haresh, mathematically, but not in architecture.

Lalvani: What Wright did, as Buckminster Fuller did, with the fourth dimension was conceptually wrong. The spatial interpretation was incorrect. They tried to interpret the fourth dimension as the spatial extension of three dimensions. They would add explosions of other features to it to make it dynamic. Fuller's Simpletron is the same. Process was time limited. Fifty years later Fuller shifted from time-space to the spatial analogy, concluding that if three axes is 3-D space, then four axes is 4-D space. Bill, in your interpretation of Falling Water, you are describing the spatial device of passing-through without touching as the time element, as if the planes were moving through (in time) but were frozen (in space). This is an interpretative spin on the four-dimensional space-time model. Recall that Theo van Doesburg, following Peter Manning, was 'exploding' the cube outwards along the three directions of cubic space, an effect captured in the rooftops of many Manhattan buildings. He called this the fourth dimension. Wright too described the fourth dimension in a similar way. It is the 'depth dimension', adding (the depth of) space as an extra dimension to the familiar three. Wright was conscious of what you are saying. In the mid-1980s I did a computer animation of a true six-dimensional cube that morphed into a three-dimensional cubic lattice, by aligning three of the six dimensions along the familiar three axes. The three 'excess' dimensions were apparently 'lost' but remained embedded in the basic three. Wright, I think, sensed this as his 'depth dimension' which, incidentally, is itself three-dimensional. This makes the Wrightian space (in the Kaufmann house, for example) a true projection of six-dimensional space. I do not see that a mathematical description has to be different from an architectural description, at least in its formal aspects. It is true that in four-dimensional space there is a passing-through of elements, but Wright's case is different in that when planes pass through they remain parallel to the three directions of space. In four-dimensional space, planes also pass through but they remain parallel to four directions of space. This is not the case in Wright. In the 1980s we did an interesting animation of the four- and five-dimensional cubes where this passing-through of planes and volumes was evident as they rotated in hyperspace in a manner reminiscent of Banchoff. The difficulty is that you are describing time in terms of space; I am just describing space. Incidentally, Fuller began with the temporal aspect in his *4D Timelock*, but 50 years later (in *Synergetics*), he shifted to the fourth dimension as space. However, his spatial definition was locked in a dimensional analogy and he described the fourth dimension as having four axes and four planes (just as the third dimension has three axes and three planes). The mathematically correct answer is four axes and six planes. This, as you know, is the space I work in.

Brigham: We're sitting right now in at least three, maybe five or six dimensions of colour.

Jelacic: I would like to challenge the idea that we receive more kinds of information. In terms of physiology, can information receptors change, as long we are here with two eyes and ears. Isn't it the quality of information that has changed?

Brigham: Also it is information management. Today kids can navigate in different ways. For example, when a kid has a calculator for sine waves, he can go to the next level, that of operating on sine waves.

Jelacic: Again, I think the tools provide not so much more information as different information. The difference might relate to the transience in culture. If this information is more transient, does it release us from the responsibility of knowing the landscape? We don't have to worry about our permanence and comfort.

Gans: Aren't you both talking about the organisation of information? Tom's presentation countered the prevailing notion of layers of information with the idea of organs of information. Maybe you could talk a bit more about this organ as a resistant, self-defining thing, about packaging.

Brigham: I think we, and kids especially, see a broader range for information, in that we have the expectation that we can change information. We say, 'Wow it can be this or something else.' Previously you were supposed to take the given information as gospel.

Kuz: I would like to go back to our previous conversation. Mahadev, if people haven't changed then why has space? Pyramids were built entirely as solids with a minimal space carved into them. Today a structural glass facade can achieve 85 per cent transparency. Is it due to the reflection of our minds or our subconscious expectations or our cultural identity? How do you explain cultural change?

Raman: I can't presume to explain this. On a practical level we can trace, over time, the movement from compressive structures and materials to tensile structures and membranes. This opens up a whole new area and possibility. Dreams feed on the current level of possibility. Someone restricted by stone as a building material might not think of these structural possibilities. Todd has been creating an incredible extension of an idea; but tents have been with us from time immemorial.

5.
Plant to Dinosaur Morph. Tom Brigham

Katavolos: Alois Riegl said that as architecture becomes more sophisticated it approaches the shapeless articulation of space. In Behnisch's lecture, I saw that we are moving towards a shapeless space. I think this is the future. I think all the things I saw today are moving towards it. And it is a sophisticated not primitive accomplishment.

Gans: You have said that you aren't a romantic, but this vitalism and dissolution of matter, and tendency towards the expansion of consciousness, are pure Romanticism.

Katavolos: I am not a romantic. I am an organicist, and organicism is one-on-oneness: hand/glove, foot/shoe, hat/head. The notion of a shared chair or common commode is unconscionable. Organic environments can touch at times, even embrace, but will never be created by consensus. For me, the epiphany is plastic. Polymers are produced for a purpose – to allow a one-on-one or one-of-a-kindness to exist.

Gans: I mean Romanticism like '*sturm und drang*'. Romantic thought asserts that as consciousness evolves so does its forms and that, as we approach pure thought, we approach dematerialisation of culture into a kind of extreme individualism. In Hegel's theory, art begins with the Sphinx and ends in the lyric poem. Or take Victor Hugo's statement that information will kill the symbolic aspect of architecture. Why build something for everyone when everyone can write their own ephemeral, transportable book? This is romantic.

Katavolos: That's not romantic. Look at Steven Hawking – he can't move, only think. He does the best thinking. I can see a life in which none of this is here. The woman on TV last night was only part there.

Gans: Romantic isn't corporeal, it depends on pure thought.

Katavolos: That's where we're going.

Gans: Then we are neo-romantic in some regard.

Johansen: In architectural terms, our buildings are becoming more and more dematerialised. Dematerialisation is seen in our efforts to create cyberspace. Kenneth Frampton will discuss tectonics later. But even tectonics may lose its dominance in architecture. How do we adjust to this? History is a parade of advancing tectonics from the Roman arch, to the Gothic, to the Crystal Palace. Each one prompted a style that took a lot of time to develop and accept. There was resistance to each one, resistance to advancing technology, known as 'technology shock' or 'culture shock.' In the long run, society accepts it. Technology is a product of culture and culture is a product of technology. Technologies, I believe, develop from observations of nature. It becomes more and more evident that the higher the development of technology, the closer it approaches the processes of nature.

6.
Liquid Villa, 2000,
William Katavolos

Kuz: What do we want technology to do for us?

Johansen: Technology is ourselves, not something 'out there'. It is our energy, intelligence, and moral responsibility. The statement over the de Chardin Foundation in London moves me. The building is dedicated to 'a civilisation increasingly responsible for its own evolution'. Let that sink in.

David: Technology sets us free to figuratively, if not literally, pick up the tents and move them.

Katavolos: The sensory motor extensions are acceptable but the mental ones are the frightening ones and they are the ones we are in the middle of now. When Timothy Leary was fooling around with LSD in the 1960s there were a lot of frightened people, but we learnt a lot. We were advancing to virtual reality then. I don't think this next moment will shock us in the least. I don't want to go to Europe any more. I have been to Rome 22 times. I would just as soon do it as Disney does it and plug in my headset to travel.

Gans: The reverse discussion would be about limits of responsiveness in behaviour, material or geometry. Todd is dealing with the clear limits of material. His freedom is within the limits of the fabric. In our panel's utopian way we keep proposing that there are no such limits; but it might be interesting to talk about the limits.

Katavolos: Someone said it beautifully last night. I think it was Heidegger. Or did he leave early. Anyway, during Behnisch's lecture, someone referred to Heidegger's statement that there aren't limits there is the beginning. The boundary isn't the end; it is the beginning. The elasticity of limits is a strange thing.

Gans: Boundaries aren't the same as limits exactly, so I would be interested in hearing Mahadev or Todd talk about the limitations of the material and then the conditions or boundaries. What stops you from making the tent 800 million miles big? How would Ahmet talk about the boundaries or organisms? What are our abilities to model forces and our digital limits? Tom, you were talking about how many layers of information you can put in the computer . . .

Katavolos: The French want to drop a cable from 32,000 miles up, from the geosynchronous limit of earth. They have tried experiments and failed. We can't extend more than 50 miles.

Brigham: Limits, in the same way as facts, don't provide an explanation; they require it. An existing analogy is being tested at the limits.

Gans: What are the limits of homomorphism? You said that you can't go through zero because it's cheating.

Brigham: That means we should maintain some thing throughout, to make an analogy.

Gans: So that's a cognitive limit.

Brigham: Cognitive limits are interesting.

Dalland: Scale. Let's say we can span 1000 feet and we can put a small town under there as an encapsulated environment. Who's interested — Disney and entertainment. When will a real town want it? Maybe five years from now. So far nobody has wanted it. I don't see technology as being the limiting factor.

Johansen: Mahadev, how would you deal with a dome like Fuller's over New York?

Raman: You do get scale effects. You can't take a small space and move it to a site the size of New York and expect the environment to behave the same way. A space like we are in will have an average humidity and a uniform temperature; but critically large volumes have climates in themselves so they might even get weather systems. You start to get this kind of situation at Kansai and Phoenix, with huge differences in temperature and air velocities across the spaces. In Phoenix, there are even clouds in part of the building — which are intentional. At the scale of New York City, the solar radiation differential from east to west face could drive elements within the space so that there might actually be thunderstorms inside. We haven't explored these situations but we have the wherewithal to explore them if it were necessary.

Dalland: If the roof is large enough and translucent enough, solar gain could heat the interior air and cause it to want to rise and expand. The upward force of the heated air could be used to hold the roof up.

Katavolos: You'd have to tie the building down . . .

7.
**Donna Karan Design
Studio, 1996, FTL**

Photo credit:
Elliot Kaufman

Raman: This discussion counters the perception that our world will become more virtual and that we will be wandering around in it as an avatar of ourselves.

Gans: This is a wonderful discussion and like Kiesler's house endless. But we have a lecture in 20 minutes so we'll have to stop.

Part III

Organ-i-city

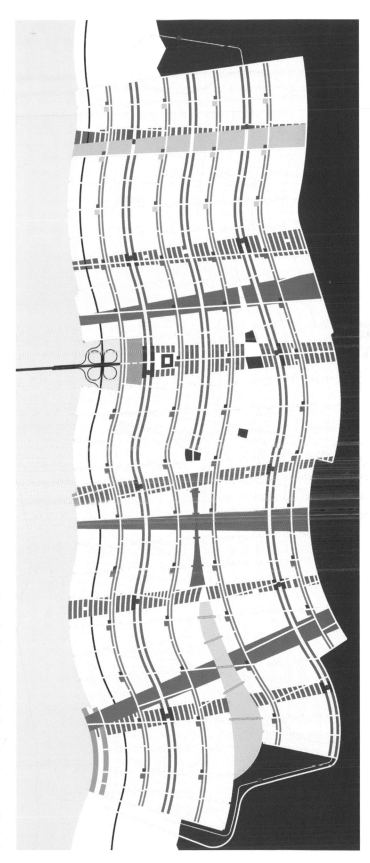

Pedestrian City for 300,000 from Housing the Next Ten Million, Gans & Jelacic. Positioned on the hillside rim of the Great Central Valley of California, the city has overlapping spatial and neighbourhood structures: one based on a 1/4 mile radial walk to school, a second based on a system of soft or green ways running from mountain to valley as water conduits, and a third based on bands of public and commercial intensity that alternate formally with the greenways. The town belongs to a network of like cities along the valley rim, connected to each other and the pre-existing metropolis by vehicular and high speed rail routes

1 4

John Johansen

Organic Contexts

In our organic approach it is important to mention that those in various fields of endeavour other than physicists share in this new way of thinking; which is to say that we can now see ourselves and our earth somewhat differently. I refer you to a valuable book by Fritjof Capra entitled *The Turning Point*.[1] In one chapter, 'The New Paradigm', he states that we have discarded the machine in favour of the organism as a model. He sees the new view of ourselves and the earth as organic, ecological and holistic. This view has taken hold and measurably affected our thinking in the arts, sciences, communications and philosophy, and will surely affect architecture as well.

Observations by others reinforce this position. The British futurist John McHale saw industrial design as the process of design, production, marketing, feedback and redesign in the biological terms of 'metabolism'. He began to apply new terminology, which psychologically brought him to think differently. John Galbraith, the well-known economist and author, reports that large corporations are now organising themselves according to organic principles. The architect and critic Forrest Wilson speaks of smart buildings seen not as stolid, static monuments but as 'animate artefacts'. Lewis Thomas has reinterpreted Charles Darwin's world of desperate conflict for survival as a world of 'ecological balance', a symbiosis in which all plant and animal life live in interdependence.

The Jesuit priest and naturalist Pierre de Chardin reported at one time that he had no disapproval of growing urban development, as long as it were to follow natural law. An admirer of de Chardin, the Danish architect Peter Broberg, looks upon cities as 'microsystems' and speaks of city planing as 'urban genetics'. Notable research is being conducted by the British architect and computer specialist John Frasier, whose *An Evolutionary Architecture* deals

John Johansen

with an emerging field known as 'architectural genesis'. His 'universal constructor' is a tool of explanation and demonstration for a radically new design process. His computerised models, produced by his 'constructor' will, he states, 'express the equilibrium among endogenous development, architectural concept, and the exogenous influences exerted by the environment round it'.[2] The point here is that these distinguished observers, among many others, begin to speak of architecture and urban design in biological terms.

On even larger scales, city planning may be equally involved in the organic approach. For the city may be considered as an organism, with all its attributes but of greater complexity. (For that matter, the cosmos itself may be seen as an organism.) As an organism, the city is made up of organs which, in this case, are departments of service, distribution, communications, maintenance, municipal government, welfare and other public and private institutions. In terms of their human activities or events these organs make up the life of the city, the city as the cumulative overlay of activity patterns. The buildings housing these activities are simply shells – however, they are shells that should be as well fitted to the occupant as shells are to shellfish. If the interrelation and interaction of the various departments of urban activity are to be expressed in architectural terms, then the performance of each major building must follow this scenario.

As changes and adjustments in the city are inevitable and constant, we introduce another aspect of existence to be found in all living things. The city organism, with its numerous organs, will be in a state of nonequilibrium, of dynamic stability, always at work as it were. We change our tissues completely in an average of seven years. In the case of the city, dynamic stability would suggest that the city does not lose its identity, as we do not.

If we further consider the city organism in terms of this ongoing process, perhaps we will find in our studies of 'urban genetics' guidance by what de Chardin referred to as 'natural law'. As we are already able to define existing buildings in code, perhaps we will alter or replace them according to an all-embracing, citywide computer model. A city is a company of buildings in which each building could know its own coded instructions. To this extent a building could be considered conscious of its own operations, of the operation of the other buildings nearby and of the entire community that is the man-made environment, the city. It would be wonderful to have design control of a building that would change itself as changing forces around it required it to do, so that these relationships would come to be more important than the identity of the building. We anticipate, then, that computer models of this sort will be developed not only for buildings, but also for building complexes, neighbourhoods, cities and regions both natural and man-made. Would this not be the ultimate in contextualism, not simply of appearance but of a symbiotic nature?

Notes

1. Fritjof Capra, *The Turning Point: Science, Society and the Rising Culture*, Bantam/Doubleday (New York), 1982, p 37.
2. John Frasier, *An Evolutionary Architecture*, Architectural Association Publications (London), 1995, p 145.

15

Kenneth Frampton

Organic Organ-i-city

The term organic as applied to architecture has meant rather different things in different situations so, unless we specify the time and place of its application, it is difficult to define it. If we try to locate the fundamental root cause, its self-conscious appearance in the theory and practice of 20th-century architecture, we find that it comes into being out of a reaction to the reductive aspects of techno-scientific instrumentality rather than the application of technological rational-ism to the organisation of industrialised society. In this sense we may see it as both a reaction against the rationality of the Enlightenment and a consequence of the scientific reasoning to which the Enlightenment gave rise. Either way round, it manifests itself as some kind of anarchic, more natural and idiosyncratic 'other' that has been in the wings for some time, perhaps even since the middle of the 17th century and the beginnings of Cartesian doubt as linked to the processes of empirical science and, most directly, to the emergence of the life sciences – namely to William Harvey's discovery of the circulation of blood, which was a fundamental precondition for the evolution of that which we know today as biology.

As far as the history of architecture is concerned, it is surely no accident that Cartesian doubt should lead rather unexpectedly to a critique of classicism and to an under-mining of the divine principles of the classical world. I am referring to Claude Perrault who, significantly enough, was a medical doctor and pioneer in the field of anatomical and biomechanical research prior to being commissioned by Colbert to reground the principles of architecture, in order to

Kenneth Frampton

note in passing the influence of such works as Ernst Haeckel's *Kunstformen der Natur* of 1899 (of great import to the Dutch architect Hendrik Petrus Berlage), and of D'Arcy Wentworth Thompson's *On Growth and Form* of 1917.

The crystalline as the embodiment of some transcendental natural *order* literally appears in the invented ritual of *The Sign* as dramatically enacted in 1901 at the opening of the artists' colony in Darmstadt, a theatrical event consummated, we are told, by bearing a crystal into the heart of the building, known as the Ernst Ludwig House, which housed the artists' studios. This was a cryptic allusion to the myth of the Holy Grail as it had been given new cultural currency by Richard Wagner's opera *Parsifal* of 1882. We shall encounter the crystal symbol again as an obsessive motif in Peter Behrens' own house in Darmstadt, also of 1901, and later at a much larger tectonic scale in the main hall of his IG Farben factory built in 1924 as a crystalline concatenation in fair-faced brickwork.

This crystal mythology seems to have inspired Paul Scheerbart's anarchic vision of a totally glazed crystalline architecture, his prose-poem 'Glass Architecture' of 1914, which was reified by Bruno Taut in his Deutscher Werkbund Glass Pavilion of the same year. One recalls their mutual aphorisms: Sheerbart's 'Building in brick does us harm, coloured glass destroys hatred', and Taut's inscription 'this pavilion is designed in the spirit of the Gothic Cathedral'. This was the generic ethos behind the utopian, anti-industrial correspondence of the Glass Chain of 1919–20, that intense exchange of letters and drawings by German artists and architects who reacted to the disaster of the first industrialised war with a magical exotic vision of crystal images poised on mountain tops or floating in astral space; and behind the brothers Taut, the brothers Luckhardt, Hans Scharoun, Carl Krayel, Wenzel Hablick and above all, Herman Finsterlin, whose drawings and models were figuratively organic rather than crystalline. What follows in the 1920s under the rubric of German Expressionism is fairly well known. I will not enter into it here except to note that Bruno Taut's quasi-religious concept of the 'city crown', published in 1919 in his *Die Stadtkrone*, is in the last analysis the essential image lying behind the design of both Jørn Utzon's Sydney Opera House, dating from 1957, and Hans Scharoun's Philharmonie, designed for Berlin at around the same time, and of a similar gestalt that may be found in the work of Alvar Aalto during this period.

An even more striking conjunction occurs a decade earlier, just after the Second World War, when Bruno Zevi's influential book of 1948, *Towards an Organic Architecture*,[3] is published in English just one year after Jørn Utzon and Tobias Faber's manifesto 'Trends in Contemporary Architecture'. After arguing that the functionalist ideology of the Swedish welfare state had lost its conviction due to the impact of the war and its aftermath, Utzon and Faber went on to conclude that: 'Our period has still not found its expression, neither in technique nor in art, nor in lifestyle, because development continues unabated; and in contrast to the thirties, it has not found a clear direction, but rather continues to aspire to unanticipated possibilities.'[4]

Partially following D'Arcy Thompson's *On Growth and Form*, which had been revised and reissued in 1942, the Faber-Utzon team attempted to derive their architecture from nature and from vernacular form rather than from either the Functionalist, National Romantic or Nordic Classical traditions. The didactic illustrations that accompanied their 1947 manifesto are extremely revealing in this regard: out of 28 photographic images, 11 were of natural forms, fungi, crystals and landscapes, five were of the organic architecture of Wright and Aalto and the remainder were largely images of Scandinavian vernacular buildings. In fact, Jørn Utzon and Tobias Faber were interested in anonymous, agrarian building long before the publication of Bernard Rudolfsky's *Architecture Without Architects* in 1965. They sought to model their own aggregated assemblies on natural or spontaneous forms of accretion and growth. It is significant that the very last illustration in the manifesto was an iceberg set against a mountainous landscape; an image that surely alluded to Bruno Taut's utopian *Alpine Architektur* of 1920, not to mention Hans Scharoun's later preoccupations with images of icebergs floating in the Baltic. Indeed we know that Scharoun referred to his Philharmonie in Berlin as his Nordic theatre.

Baltic imagery aside, a preoccupation with the vernacular was not exactly new in the long trajectory of the Modern Movement. It may be traced back certainly to Philip Webb's canonical Arts and Crafts, English Free Style Red House of 1859 realised for William Morris in Bexley Heath, Kent. Throughout his professional career, Webb sought, more or less in vain, to resuscitate what remained of British vernacular culture; to recover, as it were, through cultivating *arbitrary beauty*, the authenticity that he could no longer find in either Neo-Classicism or the Gothic Revival. We may say a similar impulse underlay HH Richardson's choice of the Romanesque as the basis for an authentically New American Architecture after the Civil War. The vernacular is also a choice to be found as a point of departure in Paul Mebes's book *Um 1800* and in the work and thought of Theodor Fischer, who had a direct influence in this respect on the land-form architecture of the Austrian architect Lois Welzenbacher. Vernacular building was an absolute article of faith for the Danish architect PV Jensen-Klint whose Grundtvig Church, built of fair-faced brickwork inside and out, was under construction in Copenhagen from 1920 to 1940. Klint insisted on referring to himself as a master builder rather than an architect, and urged that architects should be trained exclusively in the study of the vernacular and even prehistoric building forms such as dolmens and the like.

A self-conscious appeal to vernacular authenticity will resurface in the Modernist mainstream in the mid- to late 1920s and early 1930s, above all in the work of Le Corbusier, into whose architecture it will be integrated as a latent presence throughout the remainder of his career. It will also resurface among a spectrum of Mediterranean architects ranging, over a 40-year period, from Jose Luis Sert's interest in the later 1920s in the Balearic vernacular (Ibiza, Majorca, etc) to Dimitri Konstantinidis's documentation of Athenian and Cycladic vernacular throughout the 1950s, and to the role played by the so-called School of Porto in the documentation of various aspects of the Portuguese vernacular in the mid-1960s – which brings one back to Bernard Rudolfsky's *Architecture Without Architects*.

At this juncture, you may well ask where I am going with all this. At face value, of course, I am trying to show that the organic impulse is not exactly

Kenneth Frampton

new; and, further, that it has seemingly had recourse to three rather different morphological origins. In the case of the bio-botanical and the mineralogical these were derived directly from nature, while a third strain attempted to ground itself in a mode of unselfconscious, preindustrial, spontaneous agrarian building which, from a professional standpoint, may also be regarded as *natural* rather than *cultural*. While I have not attended the earlier sessions of this symposium, I feel fairly certain, from my knowledge of the protagonists involved, that these three aspects – the crystalline, the biological and the vernacular – must have been touched on in the course of the proceedings, as well as the evocation of the American tradition of organic architecture as a thing in itself and the Prairie School assertion that the organic was the architecture of liberal democracy, as Bruno Zevi would repeat on behalf of Sullivan and Wright in his consciously antitotalitarian treatise on organic architecture. Further to this we may surely claim that Günter Behnisch and Volker Giencke belong, with Coop Himmelblau, to a line of thinking that returns us to the architecture of Scharoun and Taut and the correspondence of the Glass Chain. We may also note the coincidental affinity that seems to arise across the long haul of history between the sculpture of Finsterlin and the architecture of Frank Gehry.

Where the roots of organic culture are deemed to reside in nature herself there is inevitably a *dérive* to sustain the legitimacy of the undertaking through an appeal to science and to scientific method, to the structures lying behind the world of appearances rather than to the appearances themselves. One can hardly help being reminded in this regard of the work of Richard Buckminster Fuller who, aside from the culture of canoes, tents and kites, wanted nothing to do with the vernacular, except inasmuch as his favourite neologism *dymaxion*, meaning 'maximum advantage gain for minimum energy input', could be adduced as the essential principle generating all vernacular form from igloos to tepees, to yurts, etc. Fuller's Archimedian obsessions with triangular and tetrahedral geometry (influential surely to a degree on the work of both the later Wright and Louis Kahn among others) was to find its *post facto* legitimacy, as it were, in the subatomic world of 'spheres in closest packaging' as these were found to align themselves with tetrahedral geometry. The same can be found in Fuller's polygonal map of the Air Ocean world. Once again we seem to be gravitating towards a new incarnation of the Holy Grail. Fuller may be interpreted as a conscious protagonist of the organic to the extent that his geometry was crystalline and his ideology was categorically anti-urban and anarchically individualistic. I am referring to his obsession with the self-supporting autonomous package, from his Dymaxion House of 1927, based on a hexagonal plan, to his Geodesic Dome, the subject of his song parody 'Roam Home to a Dome', of the early 1950s. They both presupposed a kind of moonscape exurbia in which each encapsulated dwelling would generate its own energy and recycle its own waste. In this sense we have to realise that Fuller's position was not only anti-urban, it was also anticultural, despite the sublime image of his geodesic sphere that constituted the American Pavilion at Expo '67 in Montreal – the last American International pavilion of any consequence.

In Fuller's case, the legitimacy of the work had to derive from the elegance and economy of a revealed structural geometry that could be scientifically verified as an absolutely minimally efficient answer to a given problem. In short, an attempt once again to adduce scientific architecture.

A similar impulse seems to be again at work today where the availability of digitally engineered, otherwise indeterminable geometric forms, such as the morphing of multiple hypersurfaces, now serves to facilitate the proliferation of hitherto unimaginable volumes. These volumes are inevitably comprised of doubly curved surfaces that require specific forms of vertical and lateral support that are not always in evidence. We may even go so far as to assert that the presence or absence of these structural matrices – the way these curves come down to the ground – determines whether the work in question is fundamentally sculptural and figurative, and hence in the realm of modelling or, alternatively, whether it is structural and tectonic and hence within the province of architecture. For me, this is a touchstone that, irrespective of the geometry involved, enables us to distinguish between figurative abstract works of art writ large à la Frank Gehry, Daniel Libeskind and Zaha Hadid and strictly architectonic work as we find it in the architecture of Günter Benisch, Volker Giencke, Coop Himmelblau and Enric Miralles and Carme Pinos. In my view, we need only acknowledge the inelegant and antiquated steel structure that holds up the plastic forms that constitute the Guggenheim in Bilbao to appreciate the validity of this distinction. Further to this, we need to acknowledge, as the work of Miralles and Pinos should make us realise, that the organic must entail a fundamentally topographic transformation of the site where, as in the architecture of Wright, the distinction between built form and landform becomes blurred.

I have to confess that I am one of those people who really cannot think at all without having recourse to history. I am reminded in this regard of the American historian Carl Becker who wrote that, 'we are so historically minded, that we can now no longer say that a thing is without pointing to what it once was before it became that which it will presently cease to be'.[5] History in this sense is a wave in the breaking, which we cannot see. We think something is done with and then it suddenly returns with slightly different parameters or as a similar concatenation of forms with somewhat different causes and implications. Art is long and life is short. Thus we find that organic architecture comes back into the spotlight even though we could also say that it never definitely left the modern stage.

But the question is surely: how shall we evaluate its current resurgence into prominence in relation to all the different ideological guises that it has assumed in the past, in concordance or otherwise with its various conceptual roots and in relation to the contingent material reality that increasingly surrounds us on every side. Permit me to present some of the contrasting aspects of that which we may recognise as organic architecture or let us say *organic environmental culture* as these manifestations would appear to present themselves at the end of the century.

On the one hand then, there is the presence of what we may call (for want of a better term and in deference to fashion) the deconstructively organic and indeterminably Derridean world of the Deluzean *fold*, as this may be infinitely generated by digital iterations, and more or less encountered in the spatial configurations of an architect like Peter Eisenman or, with significant tectonic differences (as I have already suggested), in the work of Enric Miralles and Carme Pinos. On the other, there remains the quieter potential, forever lying in the wings, of a green, ecological architecture closer to the generic lost vernacular to which I have already alluded and even to the Usonian ethos of Frank Lloyd Wright and to his Broadacre vision without its necessarily degenerating into the alien landscape of the motopian megalopolis – the non-place of late capitalism with its infinite proliferation of unrelated, amortisable, freestanding objects, categorically ungrounded – which, irrespective of whether we rationalise it as a new nature or as a *non-place urban realm*, can hardly pass muster, for a scientific instant, as a spontaneously benevolent green economy. Hence, of course, we encounter global warming and all the other morbid symptoms by which we are surrounded.

We ought not to lose our capacity in all this to discriminate between different levels of creativity which have their own ethical implications, as it were; to look as Descartes did through appearances to the structures lying behind them. On the one hand then, there is the de facto emergence of the *Society of Spectacle*[6] wherein the current universal sound-bite world of the media calls the shots, and where architects are brought to compete with each other in the multicoloured spectacular world of computer graphics where what counts ultimately is the image, the appearance rather than the intrinsic, possibly invisible content; where architects produce the concatenation of hitherto unimaginable spaces without feeling obliged to rationalise such exotic volumes or to give any indication as to how they might be appreciated even if they were rationally produced. As Guy Debord put it in 1968, with reference to politics rather than architecture (and this is a paraphrase): 'We live in a time when it is impossible to make heard the least objection to the language of commodity – when power because it is shielded by the spectacular no longer thinks it needs to think and indeed cannot think.'

Notes

1. Adolf Loos, 'Ornament and Crime' in Ulrich Conrads (ed), *Programs and Manifestoes on 20th-century architecture*, MIT (Cambridge, Mass), 1971, p 20.
2. Frank Lloyd Wright, *Organic Architecture: The Architecture of Democracy*, Lund Humphries (London), 1939, p 74.
3. Bruno Zevi, *Towards an Organic Architecture*, Faber and Faber (London), 1950.
4. Jørn Utzon and Tobias Faber, 'Trends in Contemporary Architecture', *Zodiac*, 10 (1962), pp 112–14.
5. Carl Becker, *Detachment and the Writing of History*, Greenwood Publishing Group (New York), 1972, p 23.
6. Guy Debord, trans Donald Nicholson Smith, *The Society of the Spectacle*, MIT Press (Cambridge MA) 1968.

16

Panellists: Günter Behnisch, Ruth Berthold, Kenneth Frampton, Deborah Gans, Volker Giencke, John Johansen, William Katavolos, Zehra Kuz

Panel Discussion

Deborah Gans: Our speakers have been provocateurs and I don't want to get in the way of the discussion. Let me just begin by commenting that Zehra and I set up this panel with the premise that an organism is fundamentally defined by its exchange of substances with the environment. Object and environment may be either natural or artificial but they cannot be understood in isolation. As John Johansen and Kenneth Frampton have asserted, in its broadest terms the reciprocity projected is between nature and culture.

Volker, I have a related question for you, if you don't mind. In the course of our discussions, our panellists have suggested two rather dialectical attitudes towards environment, one in which the environment is unenchanted, or downright hostile, as in Ahmet Omurtag's account of cellular survival of the fittest, and Ken's depiction of the socially constructed megalopolis. On the other hand, you and Günter Behnisch describe buildings as organic to the extent that they dissolve into a friendly field. This is to say that the transparency, lightness and openness you favour imply that the condition opened on to is beneficent and beautiful – and, in your projects, it is. We look at the buildings and see an enchanted landscape. But what if we step back from the project into a larger context? I am wondering, do you view this larger environment as enchanted? What is your struggle to make the boundaries of the project and create this enchanted landscape, given the other more disturbing contexts we know to exist? What do you see as the power or responsibility of your building to transform those contexts?

Housing the Next Ten Million, 2000, Gans & Jelacic Architects. A ring of pedestrian towns connected by high speed rail and existing roadway encircles California's Great Central Valley in order to categorically preserve the farmland from pressured real estate development that would ultimately become uncontrollable sprawl

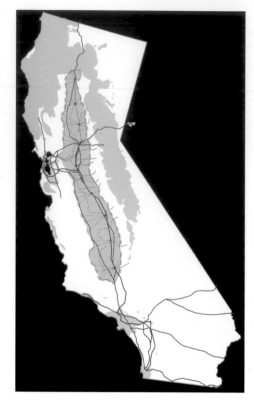

1.
Sectional Sketch of
Glass Rhododendron
House, Bremen,
Volker Giencke,
architect

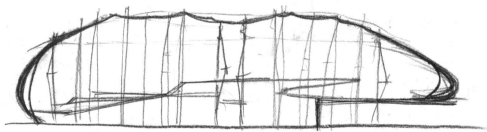

Volker Giencke: For me the organic is the connection between science and art. When I worked in the late 1960s and early 1970s with Merete Mattern and her father Hermann Mattern, who was Scharoun's landscape architect, they were interested in the relation of landscape and urban environment. And I have followed from their work. Scharoun really made the Berlin plan after the Second World War. He was an authority responsible for the town-planning department in Berlin. This Berlin plan was, how would you say, a very poetic approach to an urban fabric. It was defined by open spaces, more or less, places of landscape. In German cities after the war there was a lot of free land inside the city fabric. Scharoun's idea was not to rebuild everything but to create new urban landscapes from the bombed spaces. I adapted in my own way his reaction to something as horrible as what happened to these cities. According to Scharoun, you do not need to react to a hysterical understanding with a hysterical building but, quite the opposite, you can accept that there is now a different urban environment, and rebuild it by creating an urban landscape that incorporates the green into the plan, into the existing urban environment.

2.
Aerial View and Site
Plan, Musical
Festival Installation
with fibre optic
lighting installation,
Kornmarkt, Bregenz,
Austria, 2001, Zehra
Kuz, Julia Müller,
Sally Linan,
architects

3.
Studies for optic
lighting, Musical
Festival Installation,
Kornmarkt, Bregenz,
Austria, 2001, Zehra
Kuz, Julia Müller,
Sally Linan,
architects

I completed a competition near Düsseldorf with Merete Mattern. It was a playful project to create density without losing the individual approach, the singularity – as happens in Scandinavia, for instance. For me, this goal is the opposite of what happens in New York, for example, where the urban is really a concentration. I see an opportunity for a new approach to the urban environment through the creation of smaller neighbourhoods, more like Munich.

Another project that comes to mind in this discussion is a plan for urbanisation, which I completed while in Lagos, that proposed settlements of 50,000 people throughout all the parts of the world with better climatic conditions. The idea was to create urban concentration on one side, and on the other side free landscape. It was long ago; I don't know if it's really a solution for the western world today.

As for myself, I can't agree with what's going on in Berlin at the moment. For me, a unified Berlin was a familiar city before 1985, because of Scharoun's new centre with the Stadt and the Philarmonie and the free space, as a fragment and idea, even though it wasn't actual. He always saw it as the new centre of a whole organism; he never accepted the divided situation. Walking in the early 1980s through Berlin I really appreciated the free spaces and his vision. Now that they have started to renew these blocks it is so dense, so narrow, and also so narrow-minded. I have a physical reaction walking on the Friedrichstrasse now because I have implanted in my mind this plan of Scharoun. I feel how architecture influences your mind. Thought is more important than the physical approach to the organic.

Katavolos: It's not really disappearing; it's fulfilling itself.

8.
Church interior,
Volker Giencke

Kenneth Frampton: There was a recent discussion in Columbia about Eichler homes on the West Coast in the period immediately after the Second World War and it leads me to think about the question of accessibility of modern house-form to society at large. In postwar California Eichler and *The Sunset* magazine were able to create a kind of taste that was accessible to the individuals returning from the war and persuade them to live in a certain way in a certain kind of house, which admittedly was perhaps easier to achieve in California than elsewhere. This question of accessibility, of our ability to persuade people to live in a certain way at the level of some kind of collective policy, seems not only to be a political question but also one of architectural invention or vision.

One of the remaining, compelling aspects of Wright was his ability to create work that was unequivocally modern in its time but also accessible to society. Very few 20th-century architects (I think Aalto was another) were able to achieve this kind of dwelling and to give it a particular, syntactical form that made it acceptable. The regrettable thing today is that commodification has created the situation, especially in American suburbia, where everything has to be supposedly 'different', while it is all painfully and boringly the same. It is staggering, the extent to which the American suburban model does not respond to the vast climatic variations across the United States. The real-estate industry sells the same package, which is somehow associated with individual identity in a particularly regressive way, everywhere. This is one of the challenges that is lying here before the architectural profession which, at the same time, refuses to have anything to do with it. For this reason, I find someone like Roland Rainer an extremely important figure, whatever the shortcomings of his architecture with a capital 'A' might be. His concern for the habitat and the balance of individual and collective life within the urbanised region is critical and remarkable. It is significant that he wrote *The World As a Garden*, which is actually a record of his trip to China.

Regarding the question of dematerialisation or materialisation: on the one hand, the house has to have some sort of identity to give it character; on the other hand, one realises the necessity of it becoming embedded in the landscape in some way. And the very act of its embedding makes it disappear to some extent. The balance between the *appearance* and *disappearance* of the house is another dimension of this problem that also interested Wright, as one can see in his perspectives. In his work, the house is somehow absorbed by the landscape. It is an image that hovers between a built artefact and an equally artificial nature that is simultaneously dissolving the very same artefact. I have presented these issues perhaps from a somewhat arrogant standpoint; but in today's architecture schools none of this is discussed.

Behnisch: Architecture has relationships to all different parts of our reality, the material and the immaterial aspects of life. So one can make architecture and discuss architecture in terms of environmental, technological and economic, and social aspects. And it's certainly true that one makes a statement by dealing more with certain aspects and less with others. But that one can mix those different aspects within a building in different ways shows up in the variety in early Modern architecture, where the Italian was more fascistic than the middle European during the same period. In the Netherlands and Germany it was more left and social.

But the essence of architecture is still for me the form. Architecture goes in the direction it wants to go; we don't have too much influence on its direction. If we see the world as a unity, as we used to, then there will be a unified architecture. But we no longer see the world that way – and haven't for the past 200 years – so architecture needs to be more consciously differentiated, in more than one form and one shape. Because of its formal differentiation, the discussion of architecture has itself lasted as long as that on art. I can't discuss the meaning of architectural form without thinking of the social and technological and so on. But it's a special discussion, the development of this formal part of architecture, and we have to engage it. We have to.

9. Queens Bridge Plaza, New York city, 2001, View of raised concourse park, Gans & Jelacic Architects

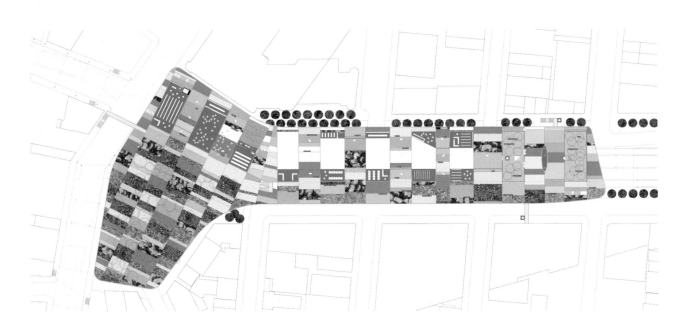

10. Queens Bridge Plaza, New York City, 2001, Raised Concourse, Inter-modal Station and Art Park, Gans & Jelacic Architects

11.
Wageningen, NL,
Institute of Forestry
and Nature
Research, 1998,
interior, Behnisch
and Partners,
architects

Photo credit:
Christian Kandzia

respond to Modernism because of the extent to which landscape is implicated in nature. And nature, as it were, doesn't open itself to this kind of manipulation. One knows there is no absolute nature; that nature is artificial and cultivated. Still, you can see the issue we were getting at, with plant material for instance. We then passed to the question of the body, making the point that this 'sack of skin', as Le Corbusier called it, is no different from a 'sack of skin' in the 10th or 11th century or whatever. The actual human being doesn't change, despite prosthetic devices and high-tech medical practice. It changes culturally and instrumentally, but in terms of its life span and its experience of the palpable world, it just doesn't change that much. Therefore all this business about technology producing dematerialisation, which it clearly does, still doesn't change the options for living beings confronted with the environment. No Internet is going to make any difference to the richness of our face-to-face coexistence. So the discussion of virtuality is an evasion, and politically loaded in a very negative direction.

As for the question of the masterplan, you made an impression on me when you spoke of looking down on New York from the air. I think it is true that when one flies in an aircraft one sees the organism, the organic landscape, and that it has an amazingly seductive order from 10,000 feet; but, we know, when one drops down into that apparent order, it's something quite other in terms of its sensuous impact on the body being. So regarding the question of the masterplan I think, to some extent, the world is ruined by technology and that the task of the architect is ultimately remedial. The only thing to do with the megalopolis is to repair it through landscape, because it will never be rebuilt. I am sorry, but I don't share the technological utopianism of my colleague Mr Katavolos, I just don't.

Katavolos: Let me try to get back into the good graces of this panel. In 1924 the Dutch architect Duiker designed one house, outside Hilversum I believe, that became the prototype for all the houses in the Hamptons and Fire Island. One house. It's not Le Corbusier, whose ideas only came to this country because of the way appliances fit under the ribbon window, but Duiker who actually changed America. When General Motors put in the highways of America they knew cars would follow. Now we have satellites and a perpendicular problem.

12.
Design for kiosk with lenticular holographic panel for "Publicity" magazine. Bregenz, Austria, 2001, Oasis Design Lab: Zehra Kuz with Tom Brigham

Photo montage: Sally Linan

Information is going to organise our cities in different ways. I am not facetious about Johnson's little house, which is the Duiker of the future. I don't see it in its current state, but in a miraculous form in a series of groupings in the hands of sculptor architects and technologists. You can't do anything today without engineers. Gehry, in the molecular biology building for Cincinnati, couldn't do without the engineers and computer programmers. Otherwise he couldn't get out of bed in the morning. Computers and engineers have made it possible. Gehry's still an extraordinary sculptor. He's got the Duiker touch.

Johansen: If I might amplify. We are in greater control of our lives today than ever before. Let me pick up your point there, Bill. We are able to project ourselves much further than log by log, stone on stone, into expressions which are natural outlets never before fulfilled, even with the greatest technological invention seen in the Renaissance. I am reminding you that technology isn't something out there that threatens us or is unfriendly; it is ourselves. We accept technology, we rejoice in its potential, we are involved in it and must take responsibility for its good and detrimental effects. The first thing in dealing with a new technology is to understand it, what it can do for us and what can we do with it, which then brings us back to a moral position of choice that each must make. Only in that way have we enjoyed, from time to time in history, new humanistic possibilities of expressing ourselves.

Frampton: I realise that I run the risk in this discussion of being seen as antitechnology. I think there is a real difference between technological maximisation and appropriate technology, and I think we don't pay enough attention to this distinction.

Gans: Isn't the issue the topical one of sustainability? As a limit to positivistic urges, we have begun to demand of technology its ability to sustain certain physical aspects of community. In a sense, Kenneth's critique of the megalopolis is one of its sustainability. It doesn't work because it isn't a sustainable environment in terms of community or ecology. John, how do you resolve the tension between technologies and sustainability?

Johansen: I am not sure I have any more to add. We are human animals that make tools; few animals do. But we are compelled to move forward. I am particularly interested in the future as you can see. I won't be here for it; but that doesn't matter very much. The compulsion is in me. I am more interested in what I don't know than what I do know. The flinching fact is that we are moving into the future, not backwards. There is no backwards except insofar we make it so; it is vanishing. There was in an earlier history a present, but it isn't here any more. We can sum it up by saying the future of the future is the present because we're determining what it will be or won't be.

Gevourt Hartoonian (audience): It is ironical that the session has been all about the organic while the panel ended up talking about technology, which in a way refers back to the technological aspects of the word organic – as the organum.

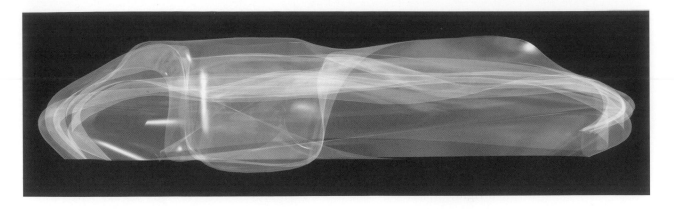

13.
Digital Rendering
Rhodedendrum
House, Bremen,
Volker Giencke,
architect

The question isn't technology as such but what underlies it, as in the view of Walter Benjamin regarding the anthropological and ontological conditions of technology that go back to nature and the body. I would favour a discussion that tries to put nature, body and technology together. Rather than in a futuristic positivistic sense, rather than emphasising technology as such and nature as such, we could speak of the body in nature.

Katavolos: Again, organicism when related to the human form becomes a one-to-one correspondence.

Hartoonian: Not human form, human body.

Frampton: Gevoort is making the distinction between body and form.

Gans: Not anthropomorphism.

Katavolos: Yes, I am getting to that. General Motors knows the automobile is a motion architecture and that the furniture in it is more sophisticated than the furniture at home. They are presently putting in devices to monitor bodily and mechanical functions – like breathing and gas consumption. A computer in Kansas will know when you are about to have a heart attack and pull you off the road. It will lead eventually to this one-to-one correspondence where a chair will be designed specifically for you, to the degree that your son can't sit in it.

A true organicism is a one-to-one correspondence. The finest example I know is Paul Nelson's San Mo hospital surgical pavilion in which everything was related to everything. Each operation required a change in the table. You couldn't do a hysterectomy on the same table you did an appendectomy. You had to change the form of everything because it was organic. Paul would talk about it all the time. We have to be careful.

I am not a great supporter of Johnson, but he has put his finger on a skin that is quite like all the other skins of architecture, except that it works and what is underneath it works. This skin gives us a way of designing a one-to-one way for everyone in the house, and a many-to-one way for all of its occupancy, which may mean we have to develop more sophisticated forms like the Mobius in which different generations live only on one side or the other without touching. I am afraid this is going to happen, primarily because we are coming back to family values for all the wrong reasons. We call it family values, but it's the lack of family values. The new architecture has to address that situation.

I am not a technology nut, but I know you can't get away from information any more. When I go into an office and see the backs of 20 people appended to knowledge boxes I know something is wrong. This is not the way an office should be. Yet there is no new paradigm. We need another way of getting the information whether through a spa or through a new room in the house. You are right, organicism is what we should be talking about. But it's difficult to define it without a new technology.

Kuz: Isn't the organicism we are concerned with a responsive mode of operation, a dialectical process? Can it be described as computing? Since technology is available, it has a potential and that needs to be tested. The primary relations, the telluric bond between man and a house or the house and site are very obvious. There are other significant relationships, which are more complicated yet more under the surface. The topic appealed to me on a sensory level, not exclusively intellectual level. I like to see a synthesis; the optimists and the pessimists should test the emerging technology as a remedial tool to restore the rifts. We have so much more information on the mental capacity of a human being, on perception, proprioception . . . Can the environment become more efficient and integral and enchanting for the user?

Katavolos: Most architecture has been a sensory motor or anatomical extension of ourselves. Now we are into mental extensions and this is a frightening feeling. The reason Gates makes so much money is that he has a patent on the brain of information. We have to move in that direction; otherwise it will be taken away from us.

Gans: It's getting late. Do we have a last question from the audience that can get us out of this double bind of customised mass production and mass production?

Audience: I have a few comments on the Monsta. As someone who works with Johnson, I think you are correct; it is a cheap way to build. In terms of cost it could make a lot of things possible. My job now consists of leading a team to build the large version of the Monsta, the Cathedral of Hope in Dallas. This makes me want to bring up buildability. How do you explain this design in drawings and communicate it in the field? In this academic situation, we are speaking mostly of ideas; but architecture as a physical art has to include stone on stone. How many of you feel that organic can become a built architecture? As Mr Frampton said, housing is a major issue. Housing was a focus in the 1950s and 1960s, when Gropius and Breuer were consumed with trying to find housing solutions. But they didn't get much of a response. Can you have this organic architecture that is buildable and appealing to a mass culture whose identity is wrapped up in that little plot of land.

Katavolos: Studio Max can accomplish your task. I mean the computer used creatively not as an iconographic mechanism. I am not trying to depress people. The architecture we have seen during the conference isn't an endgame. It is an absolute liberation that can only have happened in Germany, not in America where we haven't been through anything. Nothing here has ever been knocked down and put up, knocked down and put up again. Democracy is a real word in Germany. Capitalism exists here, not democracy. I didn't quite answer your question.

Hartoonian: What do you mean by more technology? We commodify the concretisation of the virtual image. We must address the relation of commodification and technology not necessarily in a Marxist fashion. Otherwise we are learning from the scientist, and we are working on scientific and physical thinking regardless of the ideological inclination of technology. I don't feel Johnson is solving the whole problem of technology as commodification.

Audience: I have a question about designing for the individual. I was wondering about the parallels between the turn of the 19th and 20th centuries. Van de Velde designed clothing for his clients to be worn in particular rooms. One hundred years later we are thinking of design for the individual as the organic. Is there a parallel?

Frampton: I was thinking of the previous question, picking up on Johnson. I will try to answer both questions. The idea of the ergonomic fit between the particular individual and the chair is a survival concept. It seems to me ergonomic fit becomes necessary when we are in a vehicle or an instrument. If we reduce culture and the environmental design to the idea of fit, we are reduced to survival culture. It is a different twist on the 19th-century concept of the total work of art, which you refer to, and its pathetic introspective closure which was integral to the context of bourgeois self-image in a certain period. Although it is constantly being returned to in architecture today for the upper classes, for sure, but probably not as clothing.

As for the other question, I learned something today. I didn't know this little work of Johnson was so technologically innovative. It's always worth coming to these occasions because you always find out something one has blocked out of one's mind – because of certain antipathies. I am not exactly a big follower of Philip Johnson. You raise the question of buildability and of the cultural value that can be given to the idea of elegance. That a work can have an intrinsic elegance by virtue of its buildability, and that one ought to able to communicate how one should build it and why one should build it, is evident in the Patkaus' Sea Bird Island School where they had to make a large model so that they could build it themselves. There was no contractor. With a chain saw they built it themselves as an autodidactic operation. The buildablility was built into the concept.

Behnisch: I would like to say something. We are speaking about technology. In my office we have no computers and it works perfectly. If we are communicating with an engineer, he visits us in our office and we talk about his children and his wife and his vacation, and sometimes an engineering problem. And it's a good thing. This is a good position. Technology, if it wants to escape, does so through philosophy. A German philosopher, Guardini, said, '*Und die Macht des Menschen*' (in the power of the person). If man can't be responsible for himself and the power he is using, then the forces are the forces of the demon. No one knows what happens with technology today, but everyone thinks he has to use it.

Gans: We need to come to the end. I would like to offer the panellists the opportunity to make a final comment.

Behnisch: Ruth is grabbing the microphone. She is speaking for me.

Ruth Berthold: I wonder why we see organic form appearing in the topological models in every school in the city, very often made by the computer. Students make landscape-like forms but placed in the virtual world. I think the students should ask themselves why they find this so attractive.

Behnisch: The organic approach is against the tendency of our time. The tendency of our time is against the organic approach.

Kuz: I would again refer to Ahmet, who gave us the unexpected something in this event with his discussion of evolution and the abundant production of organisms without an aim, the strongest of whom survive through natural selection. (My perception of nature was more systematic, reductive and economising.) I think our intent was a similar one. The discussion is open-ended. I haven't found an answer as to whether the organic approach is an appropriate mode of thinking at this date. I still believe that it isn't a form; it's an approach to find a form, somehow using morphing and computing etc, melting in the ingredients. I like to think that the organic approach in architecture can restore the equilibrium between culture and the corresponding (physical) environment. The ingredients are quite different but I think it is feasible to make a meal with what one has at hand and the conditions today.

Gans: For me this session is most important because of its larger contexts of housing and the city and their extensions – which are the stunning problems of the moment.

Johansen: I am impressed by the extent, range and diversity of references to the subject matter. Perhaps at times the diversions from the central established theme of the organic approach were distracting. One diversion, however, was that into technology, which is of particular interest to me. May I say on this point, from careful observation, and I believe convincing documentation in my presentation, we witness a growing rapprochement of realms of the inorganic with those of the organic, not just as analogies but in similar physical organisation and performance. To conclude, the higher we develop our technologies, the closer we come to nature.

Giencke: I am not so depressed and disappointed by our discussion of technology. One way to speak of the organic approach is as the connection of architecture, art and science. This connection is necessary. It hasn't happened in the last 30 or 40 years as people expected, but I think it will happen again soon. Thought itself is the only way of common living that doesn't disrespect the human being. Thought prevents stupidity. Stupidity is the main mistake. What I like in the organic is the oppositional thinking, the contradiction. With contradictions comes a wholeness. For me, it makes it more interesting to have a discussion between two different professions and then to find the conclusion. There is another side of the organic approach, distinct from the relationship of architecture and science, that has to do with creation by emotions and confidences, as the Surrealists say. I wonder why this creation does not occur more, and why the influence of Scharoun in Germany was so limited. Maybe this is my wish for a different concept of the world.

Katavolos: I proposed the Chemical City in 1959, and Dupont became very interested in it. I spent weeks with the chemists, the outcome of which was the statement, 'My God we can't do this for 60 years'. I think we are 20 years away now which, as Ken says, is the time it takes for art to occur. I look forward to getting some of it done then, I can't do it now. I have enjoyed coming to understand Kenneth Frampton, having heard him put his thoughts all together in his talk. And with John Johansen, I feel the same way. But for me, the revelation came from Behnisch in his lecture, listening to his philosophy and how he worked with architects. For me this is worth the whole conference.

Frampton: I have really enjoyed the session. Discussion at this level of vitality and energy is somehow, strangely enough, relatively rare. And I thank you for creating this occasion.

Short Biographies of the Participants

Günter Behnisch of Behnisch & Partners has played a seminal role in the architecture of postwar Germany. Among his most renowned works are the 1972 Olympic Stadium in Munich and the Plenary Hall of the German Bundestag in Bonn.

Ruth Berthold worked with Behnisch and Partners for five years and recently completed her masters in architecture at Columbia University Graduate School of Architecture. She acted as Günter's interpreter at the conference.

Tom Brigham is a computer graphics artist and technologist. He was instrumental in the development of digital morphing for which he won a Technical Achievement Academy Award.

Todd Dalland is the principal of Future Tents Limited – Happold which specialises in the design and invention of tensile structures. He designed the fashion-show tent that makes a yearly appearance at Bryant Park, the transportable orchestra shell that appears each year throughout the New York City park system, and a deployable classroom for the School Construction Authority of New York. He has also designed many experimental structures for high-rise buildings and future cities.

Kenneth Frampton is Ware Professor of Architecture at Columbia University. His numerous, award-winning books on history and theory include *Studies in Tectonic Culture: The Poetics of Construction in Nineteenth and Twentieth Century Architecture*, the now-classic text, *Modern Architecture: A Critical History* and the recent *Le Corbusier*.

Deborah Gans is a partner in the design firm of Gans & Jelacic and an Associate Professor at the Pratt Institute. Her written works include co-editorship of *Bridging the Gap: Rethinking the Relation of Architect and Engineer*, honoured by the AIA International Book Awards.

Volker Giencke is university professor at the Technische Universitaet Innsbruck, Austria, and a leading practitioner on the Graz scene. His work includes an award-winning botanical garden greenhouse.

John Johansen, FAIA, has an *oeuvre* that ranges from his great built works of late Modernism, such as the US Embassy in Dublin (1964) and the Oklahoma Theater Center (1970) to his current, exploratory architecture of levitation and superconductive materials. He is a Distinguished Visiting Professor at the Pratt Institute.

William Katavolos holds patents on an experimental hydronic architecture, which he is currently developing and testing at Pratt Institute where he is a Full Professor. His writings and manifestoes on organics have been published internationally since the mid-1970s. His industrial-design work dates from his collaboration with George Nelson and his own 'New York' Sofa and 'T' chair, which are included in the permanent collections of the Museum of Modern Art.

Zehra Kuz is an architect, principal of Oasis Design Lab with an international practice and an adjunct Associate Professor of Architecture at the Pratt Institute. She is the author of *Autochthonous Architecture in Tyrol* and the curator of the related exhibition.

Haresh Lalvani has applied his numerous discoveries and patents in the field of morphology for n-dimensional labyrinths, prismatic nodes and hyper-geodesic structures to projects for NASA, building systems and toys. Besides his position of Professor at Pratt Institute he holds the post of Geometer for St John the Divine.

Ahmet Omurtag is a doctor of both mechanical engineering and philosophy of science. He is a postdoctoral faculty member in the Department of Bio-mathematical Sciences at New York University/Mount Sinai School of Medicine where his areas of research include computational neuroscience and fluid dynamics.

Eeva Pelkonen is an architect in partnership with Turner Brooks and a historian on the faculty of Yale University. She is the author of *Achtung! Architectural Image and Phantasm in Contemporary Austrian Architecture* and is currently working on a book on Alvar Aalto.

Mahadev Raman is a mechanical engineer and managing partner in Ove Arup & Partners, New York, and has worked on an international list of projects. He is also a faculty member of Columbia University.